"Both timeless and timely, this [   ] was waiting for. In *The Unders* [   ] tells the truth, and she tells it be [   ] and most compelling work yet. [   ]"

—**Emily P. Freeman**, author of *The Next Right Thing* and *How to Walk into a Room*

"We need to set down roots before we can grow into whatever light the world offers; this is a remarkably acute and resonant account of what those roots might look like. We can move from our home soil, but we can't leave soil behind altogether!"

—**Bill McKibben**, author of *The End of Nature*

"*The Understory* spoke to me in a rare and beautiful way—acknowledging the pain that exists in our cultural moment while celebrating the hope present in and around us. Lore Ferguson Wilbert offers us a profound gift with this book, and I'm grateful for the way she's helping us reimagine a new way forward."

—**Aundi Kolber**, MA, LPC, therapist; author of *Try Softer* and *Strong Like Water*

"Powerful, poised, poetic. Lore Ferguson Wilbert preaches like a prophet and writes like a friend who makes you feel safe and seen. Reverent and timely, *The Understory* will tend to those aching wounds and wonders buried deep within. This book is a sacred unraveling of the truth that remains hidden in plain sight: that life is inextricably intertwined with loss and yet the natural world flourishes not in spite of this but because of it. Welcome Wilbert's words and let these lessons from the forest floor enchant and invite *you* to flourish right where you are."

—**Rachel Marie Kang**, author of *Let There Be Art* and *The Matter of Little Losses*

"*The Understory* is part Wendell Berry, part Eugene Peterson, and part Madeleine L'Engle. The result is sheer magic. Wilbert writes with a kind of desperate longing—hungry, thirsty, and violently pursuing the truth of God in our stories—and the result is glorious. Read this book and be ever changed."

—**A. J. Swoboda**, associate professor, Bushnell University; author of *After Doubt*

"*The Understory* speaks to the quiet grief many of us carry. In naming that sorrow, Wilbert offers us a rare gift: raw honesty devoid of cynicism. This is precisely the book the church needs for this moment in history, but its message, like the forest that serves as the book's subject, is timeless."

—**Amanda Held Opelt**, author of *Holy Unhappiness* and *A Hole in the World*

"What Lore Ferguson Wilbert has given us in *The Understory* is more than just a book—far beyond words on a page—but an invitation into an entirely different way of seeing and being in the world. A way shaped not by the demands of performance and production but instead concerned with the radical act of being. Looking to the forest floor as her teacher, Wilbert invites us to peel back the veil and listen to the wisdom that lies just beneath the surface."

—**Drew Jackson**, poet and author of *God Speaks through Wombs* and *Touch the Earth*

THE UNDER STORY

AN INVITATION TO ROOTEDNESS AND RESILIENCE FROM THE FOREST FLOOR

LORE FERGUSON WILBERT

Brazos Press

a division of Baker Publishing Group
Grand Rapids, Michigan

© 2024 by Lore Ferguson Wilbert

Published by Brazos Press
a division of Baker Publishing Group
Grand Rapids, Michigan
BrazosPress.com

Printed in the United States of America

Library of Congress Cataloging-in-Publication Data
Names: Wilbert, Lore Ferguson, author.
Title: The understory : an invitation to rootedness and resilience from the
    forest floor / Lore Ferguson Wilbert.
Description: Grand Rapids, Michigan : Brazos Press, a division of Baker
    Publishing Group, [2024] | Includes bibliographical references.
Identifiers: LCCN 2023046711 | ISBN 9781587435706 (paperback) | ISBN
    9781587436383 (casebound) | ISBN 9781493446476 (ebook)
Subjects: LCSH: Resilience (Personality trait) | Resilience (Ecology) |
    Death—Psychological aspects. | Forests and forestry—Social aspects.
Classification: LCC BF698.35.R47 W545 2024 | DDC 155.2/4—dc23/
    eng/20240208
LC record available at https://lccn.loc.gov/2023046711

Cover design and illustration by Stephen Crotts.

Published in association with The Bindery Agency, www.TheBinderyAgency .com.

Baker Publishing Group publications use paper produced from sustainable forestry practices and postconsumer waste whenever possible.

24 25 26 27 28 29 30   7 6 5 4 3 2 1

To Mom, for teaching me to love maps
and also to live without them

CONTENTS

Author's Note   ix

Part 1 Seen

1. Here Is Loss: Invitation   3

2. Here Is Here: Space   29

3. Here Is Truth: Land   50

Part 2 Unseen

4. Here Is Hurt: Soil   73

5. Here Is Grief: Forest Litter   93

6. Here Is Time: Lichen   113

7. Here Is Protection: Nursemaids   132

Part 3 Revealed

8. Here Is Emergence: Weeds   157

9. Here Is Resilience: Mycelia   176

10. Here Is Movement: Forest   192

Acknowledgments   209

Recommended Reading   213

Notes   217

AUTHOR'S NOTE

A note to the ecological purist: the understory of a forest refers to what we typically see below the canopy of trees but doesn't include the forest floor itself—the forest litter, soil, and decomposing matter. For the purposes of this book, telling the story beneath the story, the title refers to everything beneath the canopy. Thanks for allowing me some poetic license.

This book was written on land once inhabited by the Mohawk people, and I am indebted to the ways they cared for and cultivated the forests around here for centuries.

"A Vision," by Wendell Berry

If we will have the wisdom to survive,
to stand like slow-growing trees
on a ruined place, renewing, enriching it,
if we will make our seasons welcome here,
asking not too much of earth or heaven,
then a long time after we are dead
the lives our lives prepare will live
here, their houses strongly placed
upon the valley sides, fields and gardens
rich in the windows. The river will run
clear, as we will never know it,
and over it, birdsong like a canopy.
On the levels of the hills will be
green meadows, stock bells in noon shade.
On the steeps where greed and ignorance cut down
the old forest, an old forest will stand,
its rich leaf-fall drifting on its roots.
The veins of forgotten springs will have opened.
Families will be singing in the fields.
In their voices they will hear a music
risen out of the ground. They will take

nothing from the ground they will not return,
whatever the grief at parting. Memory,
native to this valley, will spread over it
like a grove, and memory will grow
into legend, legend into song, song
into sacrament. The abundance of this place,
the songs of its people and its birds,
will be health and wisdom and indwelling
light. This is no paradisal dream.
Its hardship is its possibility.

PART 1

SEEN

1

HERE IS LOSS
INVITATION

We are hard pressed . . . but not crushed . . .
—2 Corinthians 4:8

Often torn ground is ideal for seed.
—John O'Donohue,
To Bless the Space between Us

The tallest tree in New York fell late last fall. My friend
Philip found her.

There is a photo of Philip beside the splintered stump,
her golden shards sticking up like a coronet. He is wearing
a lumberjack flannel of red and black and stands on her

fallen body with his dog, a speckled Dalmatian named Birch. I can't help but think of a hunter squatting beside his kill, antlers in his hands, pride in his eyes, but the image isn't accurate here because my friend Philip loves trees more than anyone I know. I should ask him if he cried.

After he and another friend of ours finished their hike, they reported the fall to a local forest ranger.

She was named Tree 103 and stood in a group with her sister pines, known to locals as Elder's Grove. The silky winged seed that would become her—or perhaps already was her—fell to the earth around the year 1675. This was before New York became a state, before the United States became a country, and before the Adirondack Mountains in which she lived became a recognized region. I say, "She lived," but Justin Waskiewicz, a professor of forestry at neighboring Paul Smith College, says, "Dead, yes, but I prefer to think that [she's] just not vertical anymore."[1]

It is early fall, and my husband and I drive past Paul Smith's, turning off the road just before Elder's Grove. I have driven this stretch hundreds of times but never taken this turn before. The skies are gray and we have just driven through a downpour, but our kayaks are strapped to our roof and we will suffer a little wet for the paddle we have planned.

We park and put our kayaks in the water of Church Pond, a small body surrounded by tall pines, with a wall of rocks holding up the road to her south. Our destination is Osgood Pond, but we've heard it's worth starting here instead of at the put-in on Osgood.

We've paddled dozens of bodies of water throughout the six million acres of the Adirondack region, home to more than fifteen hundred miles of rivers, three thousand lakes, and eight thousand ponds, all fed by about thirty thousand miles of brooks, streams, and creeks.[2] The headwaters of the Hudson River are found at the top of one of the Adirondack High Peaks, Mount Marcy, in a tiny crevice called Lake Tear of the Clouds. Most of the water on the northern and eastern sides of the Adirondacks feeds into the Saint Lawrence Seaway to our west, which flows from Lake Ontario, up through Montreal and Quebec City, out to the Gulf of Saint Lawrence, and then to the Atlantic Ocean. I have heard our area referred to as "a canoeing paradise."

I grew up canoeing with my family but found my sea legs kayaking. In a kayak, you're almost eye level with the water, with the shores, and with whatever can be found on the edges of the body of water you're in.

We settle in at Church Pond and paddle through a wide channel to a larger section of the pond, and after referring to the map I have tucked in beside me, we move due east toward a small hand-dug channel. Nate goes first, waving his paddle in front of him intermittently to ward off any spider webs that might have been spun across the four-foot-wide waterway. The shallow stream brings us to an even smaller pond, this one called Little Osgood, and from there we paddle northeast to yet another channel the map says will lead us into Osgood proper.

"It's magical," I say to Nate, and he nods from ahead of me, dipping his head to miss the low-hanging branches of balsam and spruce. The water is shallow through this channel, less than a foot deep, and our kayaks glide silently through it. Directly in our line of sight are carpets of pine needles and mossy rocks, tendrils of roots escaping from dark loam, fallen logs and the fungi forming on them. Birch bark scrolls lay empty on the edge, their innards long rotted into the earth below. Unfurled ferns bow over the edge of the channel as if we are visiting dignitaries to a foreign land and they are our welcome party.

It is magical.

But it is also just a forest.

When I was a child, I believed there was something suspect in the life cycle, that it was more dark magic than goodness. I wonder now if this was due more to the lyrics Elton John barreled out during *The Lion King* than to any real understanding of the actual circle of life.

I do not believe in reincarnation or some version of re-birth after death, but it does seem to me that if one believes in God, one also must believe in both literal and nonliteral life cycles.

Wasn't man formed from dirt, and isn't it to dirt we return when we die, and yet isn't it true, too, that before we were conceived we were known by God, and, for the one who believes that this is true, there is no final death?

These are mysteries, and this is what I mean by nonliteral life cycles. But there are also literal life cycles, and I'm not sure this is evident anywhere more than the floor of the forest.

One of the saplings I passed while paddling with Nate will someday become a towering pine, perhaps rivaling Tree 103 in size, and then someday someone, just like my friend Philip, will find her too, bent and broken, freshly splintered, the smell of pine sap ripe in the air. And then someday someone else will stand upon her fallen trunk, but instead of the imposing tree beneath their feet, it will only be the rich, dark loam of decomposed life that is beginning to nurture the life of another sapling.

I also wonder, though, if my childish resistance to a circle of life was that it contained so much death.

The air is strong with balsam and the scent of leaves from last autumn now nearly decomposed. It is silent except for the chattering of squirrels and the occasional birdsong, the sound of quaking aspens and wind through the pine boughs above us. Once we reach the open waters of Osgood, we are greeted by the mournful calls of a loon couple and the sight of a bald eagle flying from north to south and then perching near the top of a tree.

I paddle to the shore to get a better look at the bald eagle. His back is to me, my view his white ruffled bloomers. He's chosen the branches of a still-standing but long-dead pine poking like a dark, wet cowlick out of the lush green foliage around. Its bark is gnarled like an old man's hands, and all its branches are stubby, victims of strong winds they couldn't withstand. I wonder how it still stands at all or if it is merely held in place by the dense forest around it.

This is, incidentally, how Tree 103 met its demise. We had a wild windstorm the previous July during which 103's neighbor fell, landing against 103. She put up a good fight, holding on until late autumn, but ultimately her roots had borne only her weight for 350 years, and the added weight of her neighbor was too much to bear. The sound she made when she fell is unknown, but the ground must have shaken beneath her hard enough for her human neighbors to have felt it. Waskiewicz says that when the tree fell, its mass would have expended an energy equivalent to several sticks of dynamite.[3]

The desk upon which I am writing these words is made of three wide pine planks, aged to a fine patina, marked with a hundred years of wear. Despite its patina, it is not a fine piece of furniture. Its base is rough wood, its legs screwed and rescrewed so many times that I'm surprised there's anything left to be screwed into or through. I found it in the classifieds, and the elderly woman from whom I bought it nearly cried when I picked it up. She said her kids grew up doing their homework at it. I told her I had no kids, but I promised I would write words worthy of it if I could.

White pine is a soft wood, prone to dings and scratches. I grew up with wide-plank pine floors in our home in south-eastern Pennsylvania, and every few years we would all clear out of the house in order for the floors to be sanded, stained, and sealed again. When my husband and I moved into our current home, it needed an almost full renovation, and when we discussed which floors to lay where they were needed, there was no question in my mind: white pine.

I like the dings and scratches, the worn places and spaces, the natural darkening and rug-worn lightening. I like the lived-in look.

It is this malleability that helped Tree 103 live so long. It is not always, as we might suspect, the hardwoods that necessarily live longer but sometimes the softer woods. When the wind comes driving through the forests, sometimes the spindly hardwoods fall first, their rigid verticals less able to flex. The pine, though, she bends, she waves, she stands strong enough to sway but does not bend enough to break. Until she finally does.

In Elder's Grove, the rest of the white pines left are nearly four hundred years old, which is nearly three hundred years more than many of their peers lived. For the first century of their lives, the only nearby inhabitants were the Iroquoian and the Algonquin people, in the Haudenosaunee Territory, whose practice it was to work with and tend to nature rather than consume her. Later, when European settlers began to move into the area, clearing whole forests for their fields and furniture, these trees had grown so thick they wouldn't fit into the settlers' sawmills. When all around them trees fell at a rate never before seen, the Mohawk people began to call the area *ha-de-ron-dah*, which means "eaters of trees." Another century later, *ha-de-ron-dah* became the anglicized Adirondacks.[4]

Beginning a little over a hundred years ago, the people of New York started paying their penance for the deforestation and rampant logging by designating certain areas for reforestation and future harvesting, and preserving every stick possible everywhere else. The Adirondack State Park was established in 1892 as a forest preserve, and to this day there are over two hundred thousand acres of old-growth forests within the park boundary lines.

This series of events preserved the grove of white pines we call the Elders and preserves it still. In another fifty years, they will have mostly all fallen. Few people even know how to find them; I wonder if it ought to stay that way.

When we bought our house three years ago, nestled along the banks of a river, it hadn't been lived in for a year. We signed a purchase agreement from sixteen hundred miles away without ever having stepped foot on the property. The house was a periwinkle blue with rotting wood cladding and a green metal roof. A sunroom facing the river was noticeably sloping, and the windows were plexiglass and rotted. We could see the potential though and could envision a long life within her walls.

When we came to the part of the renovation where we needed to replace all eight of the large sunporch windows and insulate it into a room for four seasons, we grimaced and dug deeper into our pockets than we had originally budgeted. We knew we wouldn't regret the buttoning up of the space, but at this point in the renovation we were road weary and ready to call it all finished.

There have been no regrets about the renovation of the sunporch. All year long from these windows we watch the seasons change, the water of the river rise and fall, squirrels emerge after a long winter and then spend the next eight months squirreling away nuts and seeds for the following winter. Every spring a flock of Canada geese nests in the cove across from our house, and every May, without fail, they emerge with a trail of goslings. The goslings learn to swim, speak, and fly right in front of our home, and we watch with rapt attention for it all. We have a blue heron we've named Horatio, and occasionally a bald eagle or swooping osprey will dive into the water and rise just as quickly with a fish caught in its beak. This year a flock of swans has taken up residence on the river, and on days when the fishing is good in front of our house, we can hardly keep our eyes off them.

In the summer, the river seems green, reflecting the willows that lean over her from the banks. In the autumn, she turns red and gold as the maples and oaks reflect into her. In the winter, she turns a brilliant blue, reflecting the sky above her, and then white as she ices over, and then gray as the locals clear a spot for ice hockey or skating. In the spring during the ice break, her cracks are noticeable, like the blue veins of a well-worked elderly hand, and they are sometimes loud, like the sound of an underwater echo. If you've never heard the sound of ice break, I hope you do someday. It is not the sudden crack of a shattered glass but a billowing, thunderous boomerang of sound. When we begin to hear this sound in the waterways, we know spring is coming soon.

Last summer we arrived home from a sudden and sad trip to Florida and found our neighbor had lost three trees in the same windstorm in which Tree 103's neighbor fell against her. Our neighbor said the wind roared down the river, and his home took its landfall brunt. I have sometimes lamented that our home was built tucked in the corner of our property, when the better river view is on the other side of the property, but its lumberjack builders were wiser than I, going more for stability in a storm than a pretty view. We lost no trees.

That winter, as we snowshoed across the river into the island wood across from our house, we could see the clear path of the windstorm. A whole swath of trees was down in a row or broken off near their crowns at a singular point along the horizon, forty feet in the air. I reminded myself that a healthy forest will submit to its environment and do its own maintenance by adapting, creating mulch, and feeding its offspring with their ancestors' decomposing matter. There is indeed a secret life to these trees, and what looks like destruction to my human eyes is still a part of a healthy and whole life.

In the spring, I watched the wood debris break free from the ice one morning. The water had begun its rush down from the melting mountains of the Adirondacks and was flowing visibly again, bringing with it all the downed branches from the winter, including the ones that had been marooned on the island during the low-water season of summer and fall. They lodged themselves in a mess of pick-up sticks against a stubborn piece of ice caught in the shade. Whole sheets of ice made their way around the jammed spot, and slowly, slowly, I watched the ice melt throughout the day where all that wood was stuck in place. By the time I stood up from my desk to start dinner, it was dusk and the mess of trees was nearly loose. And then, without a sound or fury, while I stood at the stove stirring a pot of soup, the logs were loosed and continued their travels downriver.

Like the debris of trees, I am caught up by the river. Some days I don't want to take my eyes off it, afraid I will miss a moment or an occasion or a rare bird or the bobbing head of a beaver quietly bathing near his dam.

There is a Latin phrase dating from the sixteenth century, *ecce adsum*, meaning "Behold, here I am." It is used by saints and mystics, monks and God. In the Bible, Samuel the prophet, whose mother, Hannah, offered him up to God by handing him over to the priest Eli, says the words to God after being woken from a deep sleep over and over again. Mary, the mother of Jesus, says them to the angel who delivers the life-altering news that she will be the mother of the deliverer. God says them to Moses while Moses stands before the burning bush aghast and agape. Here I am. I am that I am. I am here.

The phrase is used to say, in a sense, "I recognize my place and what is to be done from it or with it." Benedictine monks use it to say, "I am rooted, yet I am clay, malleable and moveable."

Our move to this place has been a difficult one. It is a place I love and yet a place that has not loved me back very well. This is the area to which my family moved in my late teens, in the fervor of my father's fever-dream of escaping the government and the downfall of society that he was sure would accompany Y2K.

This is near the place where my fourteen-year-old brother left our house at 9:00 a.m. on a rainy April morning with our seventeen-year-old brother and was dead in the middle of the road four minutes later, the wheels of their vehicle still spinning upside down beside his thrown and twisted body.

I learned to drive a manual transmission here, my older brother shouting at me every time I stalled. It is where my mother became pregnant with my youngest brother and then told my father to leave or she would. It is the place where, after I moved home from living overseas, I left my bedroom window open and the sounds of my mother drinking wine and talking late at night with our recently divorced neighbor—who one day would marry my mother—wafted into my room. And I knew, I knew, not that everything was about to change but that everything already had.

This is the town where my parents divorced and where I stood in the same courtroom multiple times under the order of a subpoena issued to me by one parent to testify against the other. This is the place where in six years I owned four cars, each one a lemon waiting for the wrecker. It is the place where I was welcomed into a church and treated like a Christian and acted like one too, because belonging was contingent on believing, and even though I struggled deeply to believe, I still never felt I belonged.

This is the place we have moved back to.

Why? I don't know. We'd long had this town on our short list of possible future homes, but we knew we would not be starting with a blank slate.

Whenever we broached the idea of transplanting from our home in another state, we would list the reasons why it didn't make sense to come here. There aren't many jobs for my husband's profession. Where would we meet people? What church could we be a part of in good conscience? The nearest city and airport are an hour and a half away and across an international border.

It was an act of faith, real faith, the sort that doesn't know the next step and prepares to take it anyway, hoping something good is to come.

Sometimes we act in faith though, and the result is a crashing fall of everything that seemed sure anyway.

The world was still on pandemic lockdown when we said goodbye to our friends in the shadow of a packed moving truck. We spread a blanket out on our front yard in a suburb of Dallas and set some lawn chairs around, and all day long in the hot June sun, friends stopped or drove by and said goodbye. We'd already moved away from Texas once before, five years earlier, but somehow this time it felt more final. We knew we wouldn't be back.

Every generation must bear the weight of her time. There are wars and rumors of wars. There are earthquakes and fires, attacks and illnesses. I am under no illusion that our time is any better or any worse than another. We have some things better and some things worse. But there will always be a unique before and after of every generation. I suspect that just as any American born before 1980 can likely remember exactly where they were when the September 11 attacks happened, anyone born before 2010 will remember where they were in 2020.

The answer, for most of us, is at home.

And so we left one home and headed to another.

While the world was still sheltering in place and sewing masks out of fabric scraps and hoarding hand sanitizer, we were sheltering in student housing in our new (my old) college town, renovating our new property by day and night. I spent hours painting, hammering, and caulking, while our contractor broke through ceilings and walls and healed our house from the inside out. The two of us worked mostly in silence for almost three months, Nate joining me after his workday was finished.

We moved in by the beginning of September, sans appliances but at least surrounded by freshly painted walls, oiled floors, and an intact roof. There were about two months of an almost idyllic perfect peace before the 2020 election was held.

Despite the lockdowns—or enhanced by them—it was already a tumultuous year. Tensions were high everywhere, and in the absence of any healthy social outlets for most of the world, opinions were raucous and riots were often. Already strong opinions about the pandemic, masking, vaccines, the World Health Organization, policing, schooling, shootings, politics, abortion, Supreme Court nominations, the death penalty, racism, politicians and character, church openings or closings, conspiracy theories, and more were heightened and drove people into frenzies about everything. It all seemed like every decision was between life and death—and because it literally *was* life and death for *someone somewhere*, it felt like no matter what one did or said, someone was going to be crushed beneath the fury.

No one was going to make it through 2020 unscathed. No one.

We were all so spiritually dry and lonely and isolated that year that the election was like a lightning rod in the middle of a parched forest. Everything was getting burned somehow or somewhere. It didn't matter how much you doused yourself with truth or how many protective ditches you dug, you were getting incinerated too.

I thought surely I would see the lightning coming in advance, but there was no warning at all. An email arrived in my inbox from an old friend, someone who had been dear to me for years. When we were last together, I had made an offhand comment about a pastor who had not only endorsed a reprehensible candidate publicly but also posted his endorsement on my social media page for all my readers to see.

I deleted his post because I felt so strongly that his candidate was responsible for division in our country and didn't want an endorsement on my page. And even though the comment was gone, I was still irked by the situation as well as by this pastor's public endorsement of a political candidate. My sense of discomfort, even anger, was evident in the comment I made to my friend, and they—rightly—took offense at it, because the pastor was their friend. Reading their email, though, I felt the bottom drop out from beneath me. In this friendship in which I thought there was grace for differences of opinion and grace for occasional missteps or misspeaking and sin, I was met with absolutism and accusations that still make me feel nauseous. There would be no grace for any dissent from the story they believed to be true. The loss of this particular friendship continues to reverberate, like echoes of dynamite in my soul. The things I thought would stand forever were falling down around me.

I read an article in the *New Yorker* recently about one of my favorite writers, Madeleine L'Engle. In it, her children take umbrage with her fiction stories, saying they are too close to home for them, too much truth. But they also take umbrage with her nonfiction memoirs, saying they are mostly fiction and not the whole story. It is as though the only way her words would be acceptable to them is if they were never written at all.

A writer has to tell the truth even if, as the poet said, they tell it slant.[5] But the truth—and sometimes the slant—is always going to offend someone. It is going to be too much truth for some and not enough truth for another—and sometimes the some and the another are one and the same. Anne Lamott once said something like, "You own everything that happened to you. Tell your stories. If people wanted you to write warmly about them, they should have behaved better."[6] I don't know if I agree, because it's not as if we should all go through life anticipating ourselves as a character in someone's memoir or novel later. I'm not sure that's a life of faith or at the very least a faithful life. But I do believe that the vocational call on the writer is to tell the truth as close as possible while also exercising as much poetic license as necessary (and sometimes more) to keep the identity of others and the specifics of some stories protected. In that sense, a writer—whether of nonfiction or fiction—is going to be telling the truth *and* telling something of a story at the same time. That's the tension writers must work with. The tension a reader must work with is to be aware that it's happening and not to hold too much against us if we write a story a little differently than they remember it or a little slant from what it really was.

The events from that email onward were one long cracking, crumbling, composting pile of grief. Almost nothing in my life remained the same as before. And a lot of that is because my work is to write and to tell the truth as best as

I remember it, even if it hurts me and sometimes even if it hurts others. The protagonist in Chaim Potok's beautiful coming-of-age story, *My Name Is Asher Lev*, says, "I looked at my right hand, the hand with which I painted. There was power in that hand. Power to create and destroy. Power to bring pleasure and pain. Power to amuse and horrify. There was in that hand the demonic and the divine at one and the same time. . . . *Asher Lev paints good pictures and hurts people he loves.*"[7]

I want to write good words—truthful and slant words—and sometimes they will hurt people I love.

And I hate that.

When I left this place in my twenties, I was a different person. A person with a lot of hidden thoughts and deep-down fears. I was a person who turned and twisted herself into an acceptable thing in order to alleviate as much hurt for others as I could. My parents. My siblings. My leaders. My friends. I did it because I thought it was alleviating hurt for me too, but it wasn't. It was hurting me more, and because of that, I was hurting others more too.

In the years since I left, I learned to tell the truth even if it hurt me. And to tell the truth even if it hurt others. And to pray, with all my might, that even in the death, in the hurt, there might still be something of life. This place to which I have come home is a place that represents more hurt—my own and others'—than I can even say, and yet I hoped in coming back I could resurrect the bits that had died here.

I was wrong. I am still learning that. Sometimes things fall apart and they are never put back together in the same way again. But sometimes, I have to believe, what looks dead to the world is simply "just not vertical any longer."

I lived through all the painful circumstances above, but I have learned not to be a victim of them while still allowing myself to be formed by them. *Ecce adsum*. I am here. But I won't go back to the girl I was before. I love her, I sometimes pity her, I ache for her, but I won't go back to her pitfalls and fears and singular motivation of *being loved*, which was by withholding the truth at all costs to herself and others. I am here and loved by I Am.

And even though this place has not loved me back during this move home, I love her still. I love her gray winter skies and her brilliant autumns and her mountains and the neighbors who encircle us. I love the neon green of spring and the unfurled fiddleheads that proliferate the shores of the waterways. I love the local art and music and food. But I don't love how places make you choose who you are or who you are willing to prove you are; how, if you chose wrong, they will knock you flat over, walk on you until all that new and beautiful growth is sunk deep into the soil below.

Poet James Galvin wrote that a tree's "strength is [its] ability to die."[8] Even in its death, the tree says, "I am still

22

here. My roots are still here, and now my body is broken to make way for new growth."

I don't know that I have come to see things like a tree yet. Coming back home has felt like more death than life. While I've been here, my grandmother has died, my stepfather has died, my mom's dog has died, and our family has been wrenched apart by another tragedy, this one almost too grievous to write about and share. While war rages on in Ukraine and the Middle East, it rages on in our lives here too. The aforementioned tragedy has not only splintered our family but also split parts of this community. It has nearly wrecked our belief in the goodness of the local church and cemented our belief in corrupt leadership, driven more by desire for personal influence and communal power than by desire for the protection of the most vulnerable and the work of restorative justice. Each day it is a struggle to wrest my broken limbs up from where they have fallen and say, "I am not dead yet. I am here." *Adsum*. Most days I give in though, if I'm honest.

While I stirred soup, the wood debris began its float downstream, and by late evening it probably had crested the falls in town and broken apart. Who knows where it went then. Perhaps to the seaway, then to the Gulf of Saint Lawrence and even the Atlantic Ocean. I doubt it made it that far, but even if it caught on a shoreline somewhere, it became an essential part of this living environment. Even in its death, it continued to live.

I wonder sometimes if true freedom in Christ is incompatible with the current environment in which we live, where our every thought and experience is on display, and therefore, whether we intend it or not, it creates a pressure for others to meet our idea of what is uniformly good instead of a diversity of good. Perhaps it is possible to cultivate a kingdom kind of goodness by in fact going the way that seems best to us in the moment, having cultivated an interior life that is strong and vibrant and full of the Holy Spirit, so much so that two of us can choose different or opposite things for our lives without either of us making a moral judgment on the other.[9]

Perhaps we do this for a long period of time, perhaps looking seemingly dead and untended to the naked eye and yet cultivating a whole forest beneath our roots. Perhaps. I don't know. I suspect though.

Spiritual writer Thomas Merton wrote that "there is in all things . . . a hidden wholeness."[10] I wonder if Merton would have said there is a hidden wholeness in death too. Is there still, as the forestry professor intimated, life pulsing through Tree 103? Or is it just that she will now give life to the forest floor, to the winged pine seed settling even now into the soil by her side, which will one day reach up toward the now open ceiling of the pine sanctuary, toward the sun that will sustain its long—and now protected—life?

The series of events that led to Tree 103's long-lived life were not so much intentional as they were coincidental. Even the fact that at 350 years old she remained mostly untouched was the result of a property line confusion. Did she belong to the neighbors to the south or to the north? I wonder if God chuckled at the dispute, knowing full well she belonged to no one but herself and her little sister grove and, for minuscule moments of her life, hikers who made their way back to stand beside the accidentally protected giant of the wood.

Douglas Wood wrote of the jack pine, "In the calligraphy of its shape against the sky is written strength of character and perseverance, survival of wind, drought, cold, heat, disease. . . . In its silence it speaks of . . . a wholeness . . . an integrity that comes from being what you are."[11] Tree 103 didn't think too much about being a tree; she just was a tree. She lived what Wendell Berry calls "the given life,"[12] and then when the time came, when her roots could no longer hold up the weight of herself and her fallen comrade, she fell. I suppose this is another way of saying she simply told the truth until the slant couldn't hold up any longer.

You know the philosophical thought experiment that asks, "If a tree falls in the forest and no one is around to hear it, does it make a sound?" It is meant to tie up those who consider it in questions about observation, perception, presence, and more. But whenever I think about the sound

Tree 103 made when she fell, the sound of dynamite ricocheting and reverberating through the woods that belong to no one, the tremors she sent out for acres, I wonder if it is not so much the sound we make when we fall—and not even the life we lived before the fall—but the life we will give to the life to come that makes the most sound of all.

One nature writer says, "To understand the tree in its death is to first understand the tree in its life."[13] This is what I am setting out to do, to understand the life of a tree from the perspective of what's beneath the tree, what's known as the understory. And, in doing so, to try to understand the thunderous shattering of what felt sure before the past few years. I want to pull back the canopy and dig through the dirt, spy on the intricacies of death and what it gives to life. I want to look at grief and hope without wavering, hold them both in my hand at the same time.

My friend Philip and I decide to go for an early morning paddle. After, once the kayaks are stowed on the roof of my car, we drive a quarter of a mile down the road to a tiny pull-off with a big red gate. We change our shoes, turn our hats backward, and skirt the red gate to the barely-there path on the other side.

The scents of goldenrod and tansy, and something sharper and more primal, fill the air. The grasses are bent over a small footpath, wide enough for our steps right in front of the other and no wider. Philip walks ahead and I meander behind, keeping him in my view, but barely. He knows the way we're headed, and I'm a mere follower.

The path forks, and Philip lets his intuition lead. He says it's been nearly a year since he was back here. We come to a pipeline crowded with shoulder-high white pines and balsam, birches and beeches, aspens and an occasional oak. The path grows muddier, but we keep step in the middle of the path, our hiking shoes caking with wet dirt. Another eighth of a mile ahead we duck into another path, this one taking us right into the forest sanctuary. I say to Philip, "For me the door to the woods is the door to the temple."[14]

This part of the forest is new growth. Or newish—a hundred- or two-hundred-year-old trees. Philip calls out all their names, but his eyes are peeled for something smaller, less imposing, and older: a kind of lichen he likes.

We hike deeper in, the air growing moist. The rocks are carpeted in moss, the ground covered in hip-high ferns and club moss. We are talking about a book he read recently, and he quotes from it: "If mosses dream, I suspect they dream of rain."[15] We bend down and run our hands lightly over the forest rug, and I think of a line from a poem I read once: "Green is a solace, a promise of peace."[16] This forest is a solace, a place of peace.

The floor is thick and soft with brown pine needles, fallen from the white pines that tower above us. I might have been able to wrap my arms around one of the pines or birches or beeches when we first stepped over the threshold into this forest, but the deeper into the wood we go, the bigger the trunks grow. I could spread my arms around a tree and they wouldn't even enfold a fifth of the circumference of one.

Forgive me for anthropomorphizing, but I like to call Tree 103 "she." L'Engle wrote, "If we think of everything in the created order as good, because God is Creator, then gender in rock and rose, tree and turnip, sea and seed, is a form of thanks and praise,"[17] and so I feel in good company.[18]

Squirrels have begun nesting in the crevices and cracks of Tree 103. Decomposed leaves beneath her now house earthworms and other bugs. Her boughs have created havens for small critters running from larger prey. Fungi and moss are beginning to grow upon her bark, in places they wouldn't have survived while she stood upright. Her golden crown still points upward from the stump, but it has dulled a bit over the past year, no longer as brilliant and fresh. It will take another two or three hundred years for Tree 103 to entirely decompose, and even then the new growth where her trunk once rested will remain fed by her specific nutrients for another few centuries or more.

Did Tree 103 make a sound when she fell?

I think she made a sound that will echo forever.

2

HERE IS HERE
SPACE

. . . **perplexed, but not in despair . . .**
—2 Corinthians 4:8

I live my life in circles that grow,
 And are drawn over things that be;
The last mayhap I must ever forego,
 But strive to reach it I may.

I turn about God, round the ancient tower's form.
 On æons and æons I am borne along;
And I know not yet, am I a falcon or a storm,
 Or one great song.

   —Rainer Maria Rilke, "The Book of Hours,"
         trans. Sasha Best

The winter here is usually harsh, the kind locals like to warn newcomers of with a bit of pride in their voices. Sometimes it is so cold the snow that lands in November doesn't melt until spring; layers just keep getting added. If you sliced down through a snowbank in the middle of a yard in February, it would look like the rocky edge of an eons-old river, layers and layers and layers revealing its age. On a still unreasonably cold day in late February, some locals will run errands in T-shirts and shorts, simply to celebrate it being above freezing.

What is considered a usual winter, however, has changed since I lived here last. As our whole globe warms, this area is no exception. I remember some frigid mornings in my twenties when I would stuff my pajama legs into boots, run down two flights of stairs, race to the back parking lot, start my car, and then run back up to my apartment to take a shower and get dressed for the day, coming back to a nearly de-iced car. There's a law that prohibits leaving one's car running unattended now, which is another thing that has changed since I lived here last.

Today is Epiphany, the sixth day of January, and the grass is still green, the ground is bare of snow, the river still runs unimpeded by ice, and freezing temperatures aren't predicted for the next ten days. I haven't put my shoes on yet, but I plan to walk the perimeter of our garden today while praying the snowdrops and daffodils and hellebores aren't peeking through. It's far too early.

What we are losing this year in snow though, I (at least) am gaining in views. From my desk, the flattened grasses and sculptural hydrangeas, the downed branches and revealed rocks are all gloriously exposed. No matter how much I know and believe that there is still green, green grass and weeds beneath the layers of snow in the winter, it still feels utterly surprising to me that from right here I can see the umbrella-like greens of a dandelion plant still vibrant and very much alive. In January. Just as alive as the English ivy and pothos and penny plants I have potted inside around my desk.

Last January, on Epiphany, I began a three-and-a-half-month sabbatical. There was a foot of snow on the ground, and I remember complaining to my spiritual director that I'd timed this break poorly. "Wouldn't it have been better if I was taking this break during the summer? Then I could be kayaking and hiking and gardening and doing all the random painting jobs left over from our home's renovation." I was looking ahead at what I anticipated to be a very full summer, knowing I would barely have time for any of it then.

"It seems like you would rather work on your sabbatical than rest," my director said, somewhat pointedly.

"No, I mean, those things are restful for me," I said, citing a Jewish proverb: "If you work with your hands, sabbath with your mind. If you work with your mind, sabbath with your hands."

"What if," she said, "you were to look at this wintertime as a time of nonproduction of any kind? What if God's invitation to you is not to anticipate what this time will be for you but instead to simply allow it to unfold?"

I pocketed those words and let them guide the next several months. I listened to the musical rendition of Christina Rossetti's poem "In the Bleak Midwinter," and I sat staring out our living room window for hours, watching the snow fall or lie or glisten in the bit of sunlight, "snow on snow, snow on snow."[1] I noticed chickadees en masse in the lilac tree outside the window. I counted the woodpecker's rings around the blackthorn tree in our neighbor's backyard, so many I couldn't keep track. I watched the raspberry vines droop over, heavy with wet snow, and the cardinals spar with the blue jays.

Indoors, I wandered around our house, wondering what to do with myself. I can easily numb myself with mindless activities, but without mindless activities *and* productivity, I felt stuck.

What does one do with all this time? I wondered.

The answer was, of course, found out the window. Not in the busyness of the critters or the beauty of the snow but in what was happening beneath it all, hidden from sight yet no less alive, no less important to the environment and ecology. The earth below and the plants within her were simply *being*.

Perhaps someone might say they were waiting, but I find that verb still too active for me. And really, they weren't waiting. Waiting implies a sort of in-between stage between here and there. But the earth wasn't in between. The flattened dandelion greens weren't in some sort of stasis, paralyzed between autumn and spring. Even in their dormancy, they were still gloriously being themselves.

In a conversation with author Tim Suttle, Andy Crouch said that flourishing is being "magnificently oneself."[2] I read that phrase during my sabbatical, wrote it down on index cards, and placed them around the house. The phrase became a way to remind myself that the work of my sabbatical, and indeed my life, was not to gloriously produce or extraordinarily perform but simply to be who and what I am, even if it is hidden to all the world for a time or even forever.

I began to ask myself, "What would I be doing if no one was expecting anything of me, not even God? What would I do today if there was no checklist or grade given for this time? What would occupy my mind and heart if I didn't need to report it to a therapist or a spiritual director or a friend or turn it into fodder for an article?"

The answer was not what I expected.

Instead of spending some deep and focused time in prayer or petition, instead of spending hours in spiritual literature, I pulled out a box of cards and papers I'd been hauling around for a decade. I began sorting through it and keeping the more important bits of ticket stubs and notes from my husband, stamps I'd saved, and postcards from friends. Then, in some sort of harkening back to middle school, I pulled out a glue stick and scissors and began pasting bits of paper in a thin traveler's journal.

I created a spread around a little drive my husband and I went for, a thought I was having, a doubt, a conflict with a friend. I filled pages with bits of maps and receipts and Washi tape. There was no plan, no end goal. There was only the meditative work of remembering who I am and being exactly that.

By the end of my sabbatical, the journal was ten times its original thickness, full now of precious memories and mementos. I began to think of it—and you'll have to forgive the hyperbolic nature of this—as my proof of life.

I was here.

I am here.

I am still here.

Ecce adsum.

Benedictine and Trappist monks are reminded to "keep death ever before you," and our contemporaries quip, "Live like you were dying" or "You only live once." John Piper became famous for inciting a generation of twentysomethings with the phrase "Don't waste your life."[3] And Mary Oliver, writing about what it means to be an artist, said, "He who does not crave that roofless place eternity should stay at home."[4] These mottos or quips or calls, as inciting as they may be, do not reflect the kind of flourishing I'm compelled by in Crouch's words about being magnificently oneself.

Perhaps a person can move through life, every action of theirs birthed on the precipice of "Tomorrow I might die," but I wonder what might change if instead we said, "Today I am here."

This has become my own mantra of sorts, the breath prayer I draw in: *I am here.*

But my being here is nothing without God being with me, and so I exhale: *And you are here with me.*

In a play on John's words in his letter to the early Christians, "Love not the things of this world," poet Richard Wilbur titles a poem "Love Calls Us to the Things of This World."

"Oh, let there be nothing on earth but laundry," he writes, "Nothing but rosy hands in rosy steam."[5] The poem seems to pay homage to laundry and the rudimentary work of one's hands, but deep down it's about what calls us to the rudimentary things. What motivates the doing of laundry but love itself? Love for our own bodies at the very least but also—for the one who regularly totes the basket to the machine and runs it through its wash and dry cycle and then folds each piece and puts it in its proper place—love for the other.

Things has always been an interesting word to me. Poets and philosophers have reflected on its meaning and its appropriate use. One of my writing professors would slash a red line through any instance of the word *thing* in his students' papers. "Be specific," he would write in the margin. I would search my brain (or the thesaurus) for the right noun, the one that described the precise name of this *thing*. I began to realize that he was looking for me to name the thing beneath the thing. It is not a thing that love calls us to. It is not even laundry. It is a willingness to look deeper than the surface to whatever is underneath. Beneath the motives, beneath the steam, beneath the sweat and blood and tears that love sometimes requires. What is the story beneath the layers above? If one can grab hold of that word, that's the word that replaces *thing*.

It takes a kind of work to believe there is even something beneath it all that is worth finding and holding on to. I'm not talking about things and love or laundry anymore, reader; I'm talking about the hidden places in our hearts and lives, the things we are when no one is looking or no one can see. What motivates us and what frightens us and what compels us and what cripples us.

I think sometimes the reason we are told to keep death ever before us is because life is so hard to hold in our hands. Death reminds us that we are finite and finished, ashes to ashes, dust to dust. But life, what life is and can be and should be, is more complicated, less finished, and therefore scarier to see. Death seems easier to grasp.

In the poem "Lost," David Wagoner writes: "Wherever you are is called Here, And you must treat it as a powerful stranger."[6] And I wonder if this in some ways is what we must do with the life we have been given, even if it is not the life we would have chosen. We must stand still in it, and instead of keeping death before us, we must stare life in the eyes and say, "I am here. And you are a powerful stranger. And I am willing to look beneath what you have given me, the portion of this day and this month and this year, and I am willing to see surprising things. Things that are not as they seem."

This is one story that the earth tells us, beneath the layers of "snow on snow on snow." Beneath what looks like death and dying to all the world, there is another story being told, if only we will believe it's there and still—gloriously, miraculously—alive.

I am conscious that in more-southern places the ground is always uncovered and it is hard to imagine snow on snow on snow. I lived in Texas for nearly a decade and ached for the sometimes inconvenient reminder of time passing in the form of snow. It was hard to be there when I so badly wanted to be here, in the Adirondacks, in the winter months. And I find this is the difficult part of looking at our lives for what they are and braving what it takes to look beneath them; it seems easier in some ways to simply look at another's life—or a future life we imagine—and wish it were ours. But the work of being here and not there or not yet there is good work. It is courageous work. It is hard work. And it is not death work. It is resurrection work. It is the work of remembering what it means to be "magnificently oneself."

Scott Cairns writes of the creation of man, "With this clay He began to coat His shins, cover His thighs, His chest. He continued this layering, and when He had been wholly interred, He parted the clay at His side, and retreated from it, leaving the image of Himself to wander in what remained of that early morning mist."[7]

God's work was to make us in his image, and our work is to keep his shape while wandering around the mornings and evenings of our lives. It is to be gloriously who we are, all the way through, all the way down, and to be gloriously where we are, all the way here, cast in the likeness of the Creator of the universe.

After the election in November and all the recounts that followed, our nation was in some kind of stasis. Not just the stasis born of the still-raging pandemic but an electoral one too. When one doesn't know what or where or when they are, when all that should be certain isn't, it is wildly difficult to be *here* and to be ourselves. I felt determined to continue showing up fully myself in all the spaces I inhabited, and yet doing so seemed harder than ever.

Our family has moved cross-country four times, and seven times within those moves. On the third or fourth move, we adopted a phrase gardeners use to describe transplanted perennials: "The first year they sleep. The second year they creep. The third year they leap." We barely reached a full three years in any of our homes, so it's difficult to know if the adage is true for humans too, but we adopted it nonetheless. It takes time to become rooted in place, to become what Wendell Berry calls "at peace and in place."[8] When we lose our locus in life, it is difficult to inhabit the place in which we live with peace. Everything feels temporal, and nothing feels sure.

In our move to New York, we experienced loss. We left our church family, our close community of friends, our regular coffee shops, and all the familiar spaces. But as a nation, we were also navigating a kind of loss—through the fall of institutions, leaders, and communities. All around us, communities were losing values and people, congregants and constituents, pastors and leaders. People were dying, yes, but so were ideals (and some of those ideals needed to die; they needed to shrivel up and stop reproducing because all they were producing was hate and injustice).

I remember being four years old and atop my father's shoulders outside a hospital in a nearby city. It was the same hospital one of my younger brothers was birthed in a few years later. We stood with lines of other good Christian people all holding signs protesting abortion and showing images of bloodied fetuses. Later, when I was a little older, I remember holding my mother's hand as she went behind a puke-green polyester curtain into a voting booth and asking her who she was voting for. "We don't tell people who we vote for," she said to me. "That's between them and God." I remember when Bill Clinton fumbled through a half lie on a courtroom stand and my father grumbled that character matters.

My father dreamed of off-grid living while thumbing his nose at the government and did everything within his power to make sure there was no public record of his children in any government office. And yet he was preoccupied with political talk radio and stacks of white cassette tapes about the end times. He would rant about the mark of the beast (depending on the day, this was a Social Security number or credit cards or a literal chip inserted into our foreheads) and refuse to pay taxes. In the absence of our own Social Security numbers, none of my siblings or I could gain employment or pay taxes, obtain driver's licenses or car insurance, attend college or get a credit card. As a child, I kept a packed go-bag beneath my bed, certain that federal agents were going to raid our house and remove us from it.

I was not raised in a nominal Republican home with a casual respect for Reaganomics or a rejection of liberal values in favor of conservative ones. I was raised by my father to believe the government was evil. When I left home at age twenty to go to the Social Security office to get a number of my own, my father sneered at me, "Good luck selling your soul to the devil." I closed the door behind me with a pit in my stomach, certain my father was right and I was destined to a life of evil choices.

That pit in my stomach returns every time I reject any political performance or platform held, in particular, by conservative Christians. I feel sure that my soul is still being sold piecemeal to the devil.

I don't really believe it, but I feel it, and sometimes that seems like the same thing.

Ronald Reagan got this right: there is a trickle-down effect of our actions. Biologist Robin Wall Kimmerer, when speaking about how she cares for the pond in her back acreage, writes that "everybody lives downstream." She acknowledges, "What I do here matters. . . . My pond drains to the brook, to the creek, to a great and needful lake."[9] That's true about our politics too. What we do *here* matters because everyone everywhere lives downstream of someone else. I guess you could say there was a trickle-down effect that turned me away from the political platform of my childhood. I rejected a heightened concern for the rights of the individual over the care of the multitude. I rejected self-preservationist politics.

And so I have been rejected for it.

Writing of these things is difficult because even in the writing of them, I am risking more rejection.

On Epiphany after the election—January 6—I opened my laptop to watch the counting of the electoral ballots and then watched as masses of people descended upon the Capitol building. The pit in my stomach grew. But I knew I needed to speak up, immediately feeling like I was selling yet another piece of my soul to the devil. Within moments I had messages in my inbox from friends and readers berating me for speaking against the actions and words of a president who had filled the Supreme Court with judges who would vote with conservative issues, one issue in particular. They viewed his presidency as a win, but I could not unsee the loss it was for democracy and the peaceful transfer of power.

I have learned to live with messages from strangers, even longtime readers, knowing that if I give way to all their opinions I will splinter and crack from the bottom up. But living with negative feedback and words from people who are in my actual life will always be difficult for me, even if we are not close. You may have a different struggle, but this is mine. My husband's and my rejection of certain conservative platforms and policies and the decrying of the character of our then president were enough to push almost everyone I had known for most of my life away from us. The alternative was not to be truthful about where I was, and I felt the cost was too high to be silent in this moment. I had to be *here*, wherever here was. I had to be *me*, whoever me was, beneath the religious environments I'd been a part of, beneath the privilege and access some of those spaces gave me, and beneath the thin veneer of friendship those communities gave me.

Yet to be here felt like dying. Dying to my career, to the connections I had built up, to my communities, to the stability they offered me as a writer in faith spaces, and, in some ways, to the church whose theology and politics I'd come to be connected with. And it was dying without any certainty of rebirth later.

It has been attributed to St. Irenaeus that "the glory of God is a living man,"[10] but I wonder if there is glory for God, too, in a man dying?

On my desk in a small fabric basket I keep an hourglass, a holding cross made from olive wood, a scroll of birch bark, a handful of pebbles I scooped from a mountaintop on a hike last summer, a pencil sharpener, and an eraser. I see them as the tools of my trade in some ways, but I also see the irony in their common story: to everything there is an end. Sometimes in sand slipping through, sometimes in cedar pencil shavings, sometimes on a cross, and sometimes in a scroll found on a forest floor. As much as I want to keep life ever before me, it is death that still somehow captures me.

A year ago, our parish lost its longtime priest, and an elderly interim priest stepped in. In his first sermon, he mused about humans being made from stardust, and I rolled my eyes and groaned. "This is going to be a long year," I complained to Nate as we left.

"Try to appreciate the poetic license," he said to me.

And I did try, honest, but being made from stardust is more difficult for me to accept than being formed from clay. It feels irrationally optimistic. I want the gritty, muddy, messiness of clay, not the sparkling, bursting, dusting of stars. And also, I believe in the glorious miracle of life and the soul, and it is at times difficult to reconcile the beauty of a brain and a body and a fetal heartbeat with the *idea* that there was once a time when humans did not exist. It goes against the laws of physics for something to come from nothing, and yet this is what God did when he made us. So why, then, do I find it so much more difficult to believe that the atoms that bind us together were once binding together a star in the universe?

I heard a theologian once say that believing in God is the most irrational thing a person can do, and yet, he said, I believe it entirely. And, as lunatic as it may seem to some, I believe in God, and I believe God really did create something from nothing, defying the laws of physics. And if I can believe all that and not roll my eyes, surely I can believe that perhaps the clay from which humans were first formed found its first home in a star somewhere.

"What would it change about me," I asked myself, "if I were to believe this was true?" I pinched my arm, felt my flesh, settled into my chair, felt the rumbling of my stomach and the soreness in my neck. I stared outside at the fat winter geese on the river, and I realized the answer was that it would change nothing about me except make me a little softer to the octogenarian in the pulpit and perhaps inclined to research the science behind it all. Did it assault my faith? Did it weaken my belief? Not at all. If anything, the curiosity bolstered it.

If I believe in God, I have to believe in all of God and all of what God is capable of, even that which my human brain can't conceive. "Believe in me," Jesus said, "or *at least* believe in the evidence of me." I find it difficult to believe without evidence, but evidence being supplied, I find no reason to argue. "Dust we are, and to dust we shall return," theologian N. T. Wright writes, "but God can do new things with dust."[11]

For a year now, I've tried this stardust idea on for size. I am comfortable with clay, as I said, but stardust feels playful somehow. It feels hopeful. It feels brimming with possibility. It feels like life instead of death.

In the book *Rooted*, Lyanda Lynn Haupt writes about a hero of hers who had a sense of "'material immortality,' where our bodies are first broken down by decay, then resurrected physically in new cellular arrangements. . . . It is a law of physics that all matter is conserved—our bodies return, return, return."[12] This kind of "reincarnation" offends my Christian sensibilities about the human soul and its spectacular existence as the one thing in the world that is not even a little bit like any other thing in the world. But Haupt's hero is right, from a science standpoint. Someday the dandelion outside my window will die and rot into the soil below and lend essential nutrients for another weed or flower or leaf of grass to grow. Someday Tree 103 will finally be level with the ground below her, and new life will sprout upon her and around her. And someday I will die, and it is my wish that I be wrapped in some piece of compostable cloth and set in a compostable coffin and that my body—this earthly tent—will rot into the earth around it, and then one day, in the future, some plant will grow up above my decayed body while my very alive soul awaits reunion with a new body and a new creation. As poet Mary Oliver writes, "The earth remembered me, she took me back so tenderly."[13] To be taken back tenderly—I like that idea.

It is not just an idea to me though. On a plot of land about an hour south of my house, on the top of a hill where he once worked and played, my younger brother's body is buried in his favorite cotton sweatshirt and a simple pine box. This April will be twenty-three years since his fourteen-year-old body began to decompose. Every single time I drive past the hill I think of how much farther gone he is, and yet how much not gone he is. His body is breaking down and being resurrected in new cellular arrangements, just as his soul is intact and will one day be resurrected in a new cellular arrangement that is still somehow mysteriously all *him*. Magnificently himself, and liberated into wholeness, to paraphrase Norman Wirzba.[14] I believe that. Madeleine L'Engle believed it too. The same year my brother died a neighbor gave me L'Engle's book *The Irrational Season*, in which she wrote these words: "I believe in the resurrection of Jesus of Nazareth as Jesus the Christ, and the resurrection of the body of all creatures great and small, not the literal resurrection of *this tired body, this broken self*, but the body as it was meant to be, the fragmented self made new; so that at the end of time all Creation will be One. Well: maybe I don't exactly believe it, but I know it, and knowing is what matters."[15]

Perhaps belief is the thing we see, but knowing is the unseen. Belief is the thing that tosses us to and fro in the world, depending on our emotions and hormones and the day we've had and the experiences we've known. But beneath belief there is something we cannot always touch or give words to; it is more subconscious and less malleable. It is the snow on snow on snow on snow on snow on snow, so far down we don't know where one snowflake stops and another begins.

47

The thing about being made from dirt, dust, clay, mud, star-dust, or whatever iteration of earthly matter we find most palatable is that underneath that *thing* we must always "remember the earth whose skin you are."[16] God is our Father and Jesus is our Savior and the Holy Spirit is our helper, but we are not the Gnostics who eschew earth and matter. The earth will always be our matter—this is where we get the phrase "Mother Earth" from, *matter* being from the same etymology as *mother*. Even in God's new kingdom, we will be made of earth, re-incarnated, re-formed, re-made, and still gloriously re-membered and magnificently ourselves.

People of faith believe that we are always being made and remade into the likeness of Christ. In a sense, we believe in reincarnation, not in the sense that we all become divine or God but in the sense that we are all and always becoming *like* God. Oliver ends her poem about the earth taking her back tenderly, saying she had vanished into something better. L'Engle says, "The coming of the kingdom is creation coming to be what it was meant to be."[17] Returned, renewed, reanimated, remade. What we see now is not what we will be someday.

Perhaps another phrase for "material immortality" might be St. Augustine's *terra animata*, or "animated earth."[18] Yes, we are earth, but we are alive. And yes, we are matter, but we are also eternal.

No matter how we look at it—or when—we are *here*.

I am here.
And you are here with me.

I am dying.
And I am dying with you.

I am rising.
And I am rising with you.

What we find when we stop moving and producing and doing—or moving, producing, and doing the things that previously gave us standing or community or connections—is often death. Death to ourselves, death to our dreams, death to our goals and vision for our lives. And it may look to all the world like that death is final. But beneath the snow on snow on snow, there is life there yet, perhaps not the glorious life we envisioned for ourselves but something that is *here*, right here, *being*. And no matter what happens to it to the naked eye, it is still becoming something else, not necessarily something more glorious or even less glorious. All life is sacred, and if human matter is created from clay that perhaps once was stars and may become them again, then I have to believe there is something sacred about the earth and whatever the earth has been and is becoming too.

3

HERE IS TRUTH
LAND

. . . persecuted, but not abandoned . . .
—2 Corinthians 4:9

Everybody needs beauty as well as bread, places to play in and pray in, where nature may heal and give strength to body and soul alike.

—John Muir, *The Yosemite*

It is a snowy day in February, finally. I went to sleep with rain pounding on the metal roof above our bedroom eaves and woke up to a thin blanket of wet snow coating everything. Wet snow is our least favorite to shovel and drive through, but it is my favorite to be homebound in. It clings to the stalks of tall grass and the leftover leaves still hanging on, it piles up neatly along the railing of our porch, and it makes crisp outlines of every tree on the island across the river from our house. Poet Stanley Plumly calls the forest like this "Gothic with winter,"[1] and I love this picture. It is a black and white and gray world outside my window, and I am glad not to be out in it.

I do need to be out in it though. I pull my boots on and zip up my coat and let our dog, Harper, out the front door. As she runs circles around me, stopping mid-run to bury her nose in the snow after some scent unknown to me, I notice how clean everything looks. The path to our porch that was muddy just yesterday, clean. The pile of plowed snow at the end of our dead-end road, clean. The bank of the river beside me, just yesterday a mucky mess of slush and sticks and a branch that fell from our neighbor's tree last week, clean.

Of course, barely an inch below all this beautiful and heavy white, the muck and mud and sand are still there, but the snow *looks* clean, feels fresh. It reflects the midwinter light into our home, keeping me from my daily circulation of turning on every single lamp in the house by noon. Just one inch of snow feels like it's changed everything, and yet it's hardly changed anything. It's a whitewashed facade. It's true and also at the same time not true.

Peter Wohlleben tells a story in his introduction to *The Hidden Life of Trees* about how the wolf population disappeared from Yellowstone National Park in 1920, and for seventy years the park's ecosystem was in disarray.[2] But after an initiative to restore the land brought wolves back, the land began to flourish again. Why? Because the wolves kept the elk population in check and on the move, and this in turn helped the land to heal, the trees to flourish, the plant life to return, and balance to be restored among the critters that cultivate the land. The land knows it needs what humans view as an enemy. The land knows itself better than we know it.

This story interests me because a friend of ours is involved in an initiative to return wolves to the Adirondacks, and every update brings me joy. We thought we were protecting the land by removing wolves from it, but like so many things, we got it wrong.

For over a hundred years, the caretakers and rangers have been protecting the land around me, preserving it and rehabilitating it. When we hike, there are signs saying to stay on the path—in knee-deep mud if necessary—to keep the path narrow and protect the forest floor. There are strict building codes for landowners within the Adirondack Park and stringent restrictions on logging, hunting, and fishing. If you want to hike one of the more popular peaks during the summer months, you have to register first or there will be a ticket on your car when you return.

These are hotly contested constrictions. Some locals grumble about government overreach, and tourists feel personally affronted when their vacations are met with restrictions. Other locals pass around petitions and make pledges and affix stickers declaring allegiance to one side or another onto their bumpers alongside the familiar Adirondack "Forever Wild" slogan stickers.

Our congressional district has been a particularly visible and dramatic one over the last several years, partially because of this question: To whom does this land belong? It's an interesting question, and I don't think the answer would make anyone anywhere completely happy. From where I sit, this land has belonged to my husband and me, the people we bought it from, the state of New York, German immigrants, Irish ones, the Mohawk and other Native American people, and before then who knows. To whom did it belong, and does that mean it will always belong to them in some way? It's not an easy question with an easy answer.

Some ecologists might say the land belongs to itself. But some theologians who believe in the creation mandate—to be fruitful and multiply, subdue the land and fill it—may argue the land belongs to the people who care for and cultivate it, whoever they are. Or they may argue it only and ever belongs to their God.

I think the answer is a little of both and a little of neither.

The question of ownership over something so vast and intricate as land is one that cannot be answered in deeds and bills of sale, or in time or space occupied. Do we own the house in which we live or does the bank, who still holds half the mortgage? Do we own the land on which our house stands or does the city, who has the right to plow through our front yard and dig up the pipes that run parallel to the river any time they want? Does the city own the land they can dig up or claim any time they want or does our state's government, who once parceled off bits of land rightfully belonging to its Native inhabitants to give to new immigrants? Or perhaps the land belongs to our country, a place that prides itself on being "the land of the free and the home of the brave" and yet who wrenched home out from under the feet of her Indigenous people, calling their persons a problem and relegating them to reservations and state schools where freedom was restricted to a white man's way. Perhaps the land belongs to those who lived on her and loved her and cared for her fragile ecosystem for thousands of years. But who before them? To whom does the land belong originally?

Robin Wall Kimmerer, biologist and author of *Braiding Sweetgrass*, writes, "In some Native languages, the term for plants translates to 'those who take care of us.'"[3] Perhaps the earth does belong to itself because it is the only thing that takes care of *who*ever inhabits it, *when*ever they do. The earth keeps on giving, in spite of—though not ignorant of—the drama unfolding upon her.

Or perhaps it is something—someone—else entirely to whom the earth belongs. In an observation commonly attributed to St. John of Damascus, we are offered this image, "The whole earth is a living icon of the face of God."

I have always had a complex relationship with icons. I grew up surrounded by the vestiges of my parents' Catholic upbringings, including their newly zealous rejection of the icons with which they grew up. I was taught a cross should never hold an image of Christ's body because he has been resurrected and is no longer on the cross. I was taught that having an image of Mary was idolatrous and that the stories depicted in stained-glass windows were somehow sacrilegious—confusingly, the stories depicted in my children's Bible were not. The idea of sainted individuals was taught to be abhorrent, particularly if they were imaged with gold-rimmed halos depicting their divineness. It was not just a Protestant protest though that made me uncomfortable with icons. It was also their history in the Roman Catholic Church and its part in atrocities the world over.

A few years ago, Nate and I vacationed for a week in Santa Fe, New Mexico. Some friends had been and said we would love it. They were right, and since then we've told everyone we know to go at some point in their life. If a place can feel sacred, Santa Fe does.

Santa Fe is home to the oldest church in the United States, San Miguel Chapel, an unassuming terracotta adobe with a small cross atop it. Within it, the walls are lined with the stations of the cross, and near the front is a floor to ceiling painting of revered saints. The floor is crooked, the rafters above are tilted, and it costs tourists a dollar to enter. It smells like old wood and clay.

Nearby is the Loretta Chapel, another smallish church, this one a bit more ornamental and Gothic. Within the Loretta is a famous spiral staircase with expert—and mysterious—craftsmanship. The exit is through a gift shop, proliferated with small plastic mementos, icons, and other paraphernalia. A donation of five dollars is requested.

Theologians, artists, and spiritual people of every flavor have always had an interest in liminal space or what some call a "thin space." We all have them in our lives, sometimes physical spaces and sometime certain times of our lives. A liminal space is a transitional space. One might think of it as a threshold or a doorway. Some define it as a place that evokes a feeling of incompleteness or a sense of dissonance: an endless hallway, a room of mirrors, an empty playground, a space in a graveyard where there are, as yet, no graves. It is often a space that reminds us of something of great importance: our life, our death, our failures, our hopes, our fears.

There are a few liminal spaces in my life. The first is a retreat in the hill country of Texas. I define it as liminal first because there is hardly any love in my heart for the land of Texas. I prefer the lush green of the Northeast to the dusty landscape of the Southwest, and so my love for this place feels deeply counterintuitive. But it is also liminal because I have never left there without something significant having been crossed over in my life. For some reason, it is a place I can hear God or hear my own self or, at the very least, silence everything else that clamors to be heard normally.

Another liminal space for me is a small courtyard in Jerusalem where on one side is a small stone chapel and on the other are the pools of Bethesda. On long drives cross-country in a car by myself, I find a thin space. On a small lake in the middle of the Adirondacks there is liminal space too.

These spaces are not common, nor are they easy to find. In fact, one does not *find* a thin space as much as one finds oneself already *in* one. One cannot plan for a thin space or find a liminal space on a map. We do not set out with a destination, sure it will become a liminal space for us. These spaces often surprise us, and sometimes we don't even know they are significant until years later. I look back now and realize my first time at the hill country retreat was when I made the decision to break an engagement that was eating me from the inside out. I couldn't have known that when I first eased my car down into the canyon and through the Frio River to the lodge.

What makes a liminal space so important is that it is a place where we find peace within the dissonance. We know we have found one of these spaces when we can hold two competing truths in one hand, or when we can feel both profound grief and profound hope at the same time, or when we can face a truth we've tried to ignore in fear and it brings relief, not horror. These spaces are *kairos* spaces, places in time that transcend time.

On our last night in Santa Fe, after a nearly perfect week of wandering through art galleries, driving the long way to Taos and crossing the Rio Grande to watch the sunset, drinking tea at a local tea house, and squeezing into buildings and doorways from another era, we visited the last famous church: the Cathedral Basilica of St. Francis of Assisi, a beautiful building right off the center square. We'd heard earlier in the day that some high school choirs from New Mexico would be performing in the sanctuary that evening, and so, as night fell, we got in line outside with parents and grandparents there to see their children and grandchildren sing.

It was a cold November evening, past the tourist season in Santa Fe, and we were surrounded by locals, mostly Indigenous people, their heritage worn on their faces and bodies. I shivered from the cold and moved in closer to Nate, listening to the grandparents in front of us chatter with their grown children about their grandchildren, who were getting ready to perform. I couldn't help smiling. Some might stand in line for an hour in the freezing cold for tickets to the Lincoln Center or a Broadway play, but I was happy to take part in something that would never receive a raving review or write-up in the *New York Times*.

We finally filed in and filled up the cathedral, families with little ones running to and fro between the pews and the granite baptismal font in the middle. Every sound reverberated off the walls, and no one was hushing or shushing anyone. It was beautiful chaos, and it was holy.

Soon, a young man walked in, followed by another and another and another, until we were encompassed by a small choir, each person standing ten or fifteen feet from another. A low hum sounded from the young men, and from the front came sounds of the wind from the mouths of young women. The hum grew louder, and a harmony began, and then another. The song was a traditional Swedish one, "Trilo," meant for women to use to call their fishermen husbands back home from the sea. The arrangement is by Bengt Ollén. I do not know what the words mean, but I will never forget the thrumming of my heart while they sang. Their voices echoed off the arches high above us and around us, playing with one another and the echoes and reverberations. It was otherworldly. It was immersive. It felt like living in a song. I never wanted it to end. The space was holy; the space was thin.

At the end of the evening, we filed out with parents meeting their children at the back entrance. Nate and I walked through a garden with a statue of St. Francis feeding the birds and began our trek back to our Airbnb. I cannot remember if we spoke to each other, but I do remember trying to hold on to the memory. Of all the art galleries, museums, famous churches, and beauty we'd encountered in our week there, this was the pinnacle: some local kids singing their hearts out to their parents and grandparents in a cathedral that, in some ways, represented their ancestral genocide and forced assimilation.

It was impossible to ignore the imposing, shuttered parochial school building behind the basilica.

I wondered later if a place could *be* holy and not just feel like it, because I felt I was leaving holy as we drove out of town the next day at 5 a.m.

I wondered if what was holy about the place wasn't the presence of the oldest church in the United States, or the mysterious craftsmanship of the Loretta staircase, or the Cathedral Basilica of St. Francis of Assisi, but that it was a place where horror and hope coexisted without the diminishment of the other. Our experience there demanded that we pay attention to both its beauty and its brutality.

Santa Fe means "Holy Faith," and it is a place that is wholly unto itself. Artists have communed there for centuries; writers have holed themselves up there to write masterpieces. In Santa Fe, musicians finish their magnum opuses. There is something there that just isn't accessible anywhere else, and this is what I mean when I say holy. It knows who it is, and it knows it has housed both horror and hope for centuries. It contains multitudes, to paraphrase Walt Whitman.[4] Santa Fe is honest about who and what it has been and is. It belongs to itself, and the more it belongs wholly to itself, the more it becomes "a living icon of the face of God."

I wonder if it is often difficult for us to be honest about who and what we are because we humans are uncomfortable with what it means to be a *living* image of God. Alive means growing and changing and dying and rebirthing, and God is unchanging, undying, unbirthed, and the same yesterday, today, and forever. How can we humans hold the complexity of all that we are alongside all that we are not?

This is why we need thin spaces in our lives: To remind us that a thing can be true and complex at the same time. To remind us that there are no easy answers or perfect timelines or road maps to resolution.

In his introduction to *The Great Divorce*, C. S. Lewis wrote,

We are not living in a world where all roads are radii of a circle and where all, if followed long enough, will therefore draw gradually nearer and finally meet at the center: rather in a world where every road, after a few miles, forks into two, and each of those into two again, and at each fork you must make a decision. Even on the biological level life is not like a river but like a tree. It does not move towards unity but away from it and the creatures grow further apart as they increase in perfection. Good, as it ripens, becomes continually more different not only from evil but from other good.[5]

I scribbled the words "Good, as it ripens" on Post-it notes and in the margins of books next to complex subjects or points made. Every time I was tempted to polarize a person or issue or platform, I would think of that tree, moving away from unity but toward another kind of wholeness. But as we began the second year of the pandemic, nearing the arrival of a vaccine and navigating a new presidency, while we couldn't shake the previous one off, I felt a churning inside me that wouldn't let go. It sometimes felt nearly impossible to share space with friends who believed so differently from me because suddenly our individual convictions had so many real-life ramifications.

This idea of competing truths felt somehow and surprisingly new to me. Even though I have always tried to keep an open mind to the beliefs and practices of others, I still believed deep down that my way was the right—or the true— way. And I don't fault me. I think most of us are the same. It takes a lot of work to believe that the beliefs and convictions of someone else are just as viable as our own. And not just viable but valuable.

Before, when considering politics or theology or other systems of belief and practice, the question for me had always been "Is it true?" but now I was learning to ask instead, "Do

I agree?" I was coming to see that a thing could be true and also bad for us or that two things could be equally true and yet incompatible with each other. I was coming to see that we could celebrate a true and beautiful thing without celebrating the whole of the thing. That seems complex because it is, and the whole world doesn't want us to live that way.

On the day of the 2020 inauguration, I shared something about celebrating the first female vice president and within seconds received texts from several lifelong friends expressing their disappointment. I listened to their concerns and disagreements, acknowledged their disappointment in the current administration, and still maintained that a person is not just the sum of their parts. A person is also the parts of their sum, and we are free to celebrate the parts even if the sum causes us pain. We invited some of those friends over to sit at our table and share the things that were important to them politically. We let them know our aim was just to listen, not to convince anyone our way was right or to argue. We just wanted them to know that their perspective mattered to us and that we believed it was possible to meet over the table and leave as friends, all while disagreeing.

We never heard from those friends again. We were erased from their community, their lives, their social media, and their line of sight. Later, we heard through the grapevine that they said we invited them over but wouldn't let them debate us, that we were close-minded and conflict-avoidant. We tried to do right, but our right was their wrong.

On a freezing February day, I sat at my desk and made a list of all the relationships I thought could withstand political shifts, the pandemic, different racial ideologies, creative ways of caring for all of life and the earth. I wrote down the names of pastors and leaders, close friends and old friends, vocational peers and gatekeepers of various environments I had been a part of. And then, name by name, I went through the list and tried to be honest about the state of our relationship postelection and postpandemic. I was heartbroken.

Our inability to be *with* one another in the complexity of disagreement had shattered what I'd thought to be true and good and sure. I mean *with* both metaphorically and physically. Our inability to gather with those who disagreed so potently about wearing masks, the size of gatherings, vaccines, and other pandemic-adjacent issues seemed to coincide with an inability to be in proximity with those who disagreed politically. And the more we remained in our echo chambers, the more the divisions grew and the less we could see one another. Our attempt to listen and learn at our dinner table was twisted into fodder accusing us of stubbornness and an unwillingness to change. We perceived these friends as hungry for debates and willing to think charitably only of people who thought just like them. It seemed like we were becoming incapable of an honest assessment of one another.

Remember that quote from Madeleine L'Engle's children about truth and fiction? Another memoirist, Marion Roach Smith, wrote after telling one of her stories, "While all of these experiences I chronicled are true, not one of them is the whole truth. Going for the whole truth is a fool's errand."[6] All of what I wrote is true. It really happened, but it isn't the whole truth. It's just, as one of my musical heroes said, "the world as best as I remember it."[7] Even now I'm trying to attempt an honest assessment of these broken relationships, and it feels nearly impossible to hold all that hurt in a hand and know that, in some ways, they are holding their own handful of hurt from me and that we're prevented from seeing one another wholly.

Someday will I see this, too, as a liminal space?

My spiritual director often asks me for an "honest assessment" of something or other. What she means is not "Don't lie to me" but "Don't lie to yourself." Even though we've met together for over four years, it wasn't until more recently that I began to understand those words. The understanding came while reading a novel by Susan Howatch titled *Glittering Images*. I'd rather you read the book than read the next paragraph, so if you haven't read it and will, skip ahead because I'm going to give much of it away below.

In the first chapter, we meet Charles Ashworth, a dapper, young, Anglican clergyman in pastural England before the Second World War. He is tasked with a bit of political spy work by his bishop. I won't say much more than that about the overall plot, but the book takes a sharp turn when Charles realizes the crux of his work is *not* to find out about someone else but to find out about his own self. The second half of the book left me nearly breathless as the dialogue raced along between Charles and his mentor—a master class in making an honest assessment of one's self.

A few years ago, a dear friend was visiting with a mutual acquaintance of ours. I've not had a close relationship with this acquaintance for decades, even though in our childhood we were frequently around each other. My name came up in the conversation, and the mutual acquaintance joked, saying something to the effect of what a drama queen I was. My friend felt disagreement catch in her throat. "Drama queen" is not a moniker she would ever give me, and yet in the pressure of the moment, she laughed along.

Later, sitting at my kitchen table, she confessed this scenario through tears and how mortified she was that she'd simply gone along with the slight on my character. I listened to her, and what I felt wasn't anger toward her or even anger toward the acquaintance but sincere wondering if that is how I am perceived by acquaintances in my life.

"Sometimes there's a little bit of truth in every joke," I said to her, "so in your laughter, was there any truth? Do you think I am a drama queen? Or that I attract or cultivate drama?"

"No!" she cried in response. "That's why I'm so ashamed of myself for agreeing. I was lying to avoid conflict in the moment. This person doesn't know you, hasn't known you for years, and what they may see as 'drama' is actually a healthy ability to face things as they are, to go beneath the surface and not avoid the conflict of what seeing yourself and others truly means."

I mulled on this for a while. Of course, I forgave her quickly; our friendship matters more to me than what a moment of peer pressure revealed. But it's been years now, and that phrase "drama queen" hasn't unstuck itself from me yet.

I am rarely the loudest person in the room or the center of attention in any space. That is my honest assessment of myself. I typically listen more than I speak, and this is my friends' honest assessment of me. I hold my grief close to me when it is most potent, and I rarely react with strong emotions to anyone except my husband, and even with him, rarely. But I do not look away from pain or hurt or grief or wrongdoing. I spent many years trying to pretend brokenness didn't exist or there was nothing within my power to right it. But now I am unafraid of looking at brokenness because I know beneath it or through it or within it, there is something beautiful. There is a saying that "humility is living in the truth,"[8] and I believe this with all my heart.

This habit of sitting with what seems broken can be uncomfortable for some people, and it may be perceived as being dramatic, but drama says, "Look at me!" and *sitting with* says, "I'm willing to look at this, all of it, leaving nothing out." I will never be comfortable being looked at but will always invite others to join me in looking through.

A kind of passivity threads itself through our lives. It shows up in attempts to "leave well enough alone" or to "not wake the sleeping bear." We pretend there is nothing below the surface, nothing of brokenness or dysfunction. Or, conversely, we think the "drama" is what's on top, what's visible, the thin layer of snow covering over muddy walkways. We think it's the glittering image, the ways we see ourselves and the selves we want others to see when they look at us. But the real drama plays out when we take what's on top and what's on the bottom and look at them both truthfully and wholly, just as they are.

The beauty of land that belongs to itself is that it tells the whole story, leaving nothing out. Dig through the earth outside your home and you will learn a story. Dynamite through a rock outcrop and you will see the striations of eons. Cut down a tree and you will see the rings of earlywood and latewood telling the story of wet years and dry ones, three hundred years back. The land does not lie to its inhabitants. It does not keep secrets. It is not at war with itself. It does not pretend to be anything except what it is. It cannot be anything other than the truth.

In *The Body Keeps the Score*, renowned psychologist Bessel van der Kolk writes, "As long as you keep secrets and suppress information, you are fundamentally at war with yourself."[9] If this is true, then it is no wonder we humans have been at war with one another since the beginning of time over the land beneath our feet. From the moment Adam and Eve were banished from Eden, we have been trying to find a way to lay down our arms and come home.

In the poem "To Think of the Life of a Man," Wendell Berry writes, "It seems too difficult and rare to think of the life of a man grown whole in the world at peace and in place,"[10] and I suspect we all struggle to enter this difficulty. We have all grown whole in a world that will not let us be "at peace and in place," not ever.

Psalm 24:1 says, "The earth is the LORD's, and everything in it," and while I know that means you and I and the ground beneath us all belong to God, at first it has to mean we belong to ourselves—that we acknowledge who we are and who we are not. Adam and Eve's original sin was not that they disobeyed God but that they wanted to be *like God*, but who could fault them? Who doesn't want to be god of their own life?

To belong to God means to stand where we are and say, "This is who I am and *all* of who I am." But to belong to God also means to say, "This is who I am not and who I relinquish the need to be."

There is something of the holy in a space like that. Something of the liminal space. Lyanda Lynn Haupt quotes Trappist monk Brother David Steindl-Rast, saying:

The passage in Exodus continues: "Shed your shoes; *this is holy ground*." We tend to think this means that Moses is to remove his shoes *because* the ground is holy, a matter of respect or humility, perhaps, as one is asked to remove shoes when entering certain mosques or temples. But according to Brother David, the rabbinic scholars he has spoken with insist that it is the other way around: "When you take off your shoes, you will *notice* this is holy ground! . . . Because what prevents you from seeing that it's holy ground is the dead skin you have to shed." It's only our own limited thinking . . . that keeps us from the apprehension: *we are always standing on holy ground.*[11]

In another poem, Berry writes, "There are no unsacred places, only sacred and desecrated places."[12] It is pristine or amok, but either way it's holy ground, and we will find something beautiful there. It belongs to you or me or the city or the state or the church or the Native people or the chipmunks or the elk or the wolves or the grasses and trees and rocks, but it's holy ground all the same because it belongs to itself and therefore it belongs to God.

PART 2

UNSEEN

4

HERE IS HURT

SOIL

. . . struck down, but not destroyed.

—2 Corinthians 4:9

Have you reckon'd a thousand acres much?
Have you reckon'd the earth much?

—Walt Whitman, "Song of Myself"

There is an artist who has a collection of small bottles with cork lids, each one labeled with a location around the world. Inside each bottle is ordinary soil. The contents are green and gold and red and black and white and gray and brown and almost blue.

Someone once told me nothing from nature is blue, and I wondered if they'd ever looked up and seen the sky like it is today, bold and brilliant. I wondered if they'd never seen a forget-me-not or the bud of a Siberian squill just before it blooms. Had they never stood on the bank of a rushing river tumbling over rocks, clear and cold and turquoise blue? Blue is everywhere. Even in the artist's bottles of plain, ordinary soil collected from all over the earth. I envy this artist's bottles and want to buy a box of my own for an upcoming trip across the United States.

When God tells Abraham that his descendants will be as many as the stars or the grains of sand, I wonder if Abraham knew then that they would be not only as many but also as diverse. My mother lives on the white coast of the Gulf of Mexico, on sand they call sugar. I have lived in Central America and dug my toes into sand blacker than tar. I have walked on the Atlantic coast, its pebble sand like massaging balls on my feet. I live in a place now that is famous for its red sandstone; sometimes, when our walkway steps chip off into miniscule particles, I imagine a whole landscape of chalky red sand, as if we were sinking into a red velvet cake or standing on the lip of a rose, that soft, that decadent.

A few months ago, I watched a documentary about a community that lives in a small island port in Alaska. Most of them call themselves self-sufficient, but one neighbor cuts firewood for an elderly inhabitant, another fishes for halibut and shares with the community, and another teaches a new transplant how to hunt. Is anyone truly self-sufficient?

The community is surrounded by tempestuous salt water and forests, but the land itself isn't good for gardening, and so one member creates his greenhouse garden with bins of soil he makes himself.

There is no landscape store nearby to buy bags of supplements or a neighbor who can truck over a load of dirt, so this man piles five-gallon buckets in his dingy and circumnavigates the island in search of ingredients. Kelp from the sea. Sand from the shore. Some fish guts. He mixes all this with soil from his own land to grow potatoes, carrots, and fresh greens. He calls himself a soil farmer.

I heard a farmer say once that "if you take care of the soil, the soil will take care of you." I believe that's true, but there is a lot of soil to care for and not so many of us who take care of it, so the odds don't seem much in our favor.

In some ways, soil has been more resilient than almost anything on earth. But even resilient things sometimes fall apart.

The snow has been melting all week, and green grass and bits of last year's leaves are poking through. I am vigilant in my check for snowdrops, both wanting the plants to come up because they are the first sign of real spring and not wanting them to come up because I've lived here long enough to know a melt in late February is just a tease. I stand with my bare feet in our yard though, letting the damp and cold soil reinvigorate me.

It is almost Lent. Next week we will burn the palms from last Easter and offer up our foreheads to be marked with their ashes. A reminder that dust we are and to dust we will return. Dust being a more poetic way of saying plain old ordinary dirt. Ashes being a reminder that we are mortal.

Another ingredient the soil farmer adds to his pot of dirt soup: ashes.

In the span of one year, Nate and I married, moved cross-country, experienced a church division, and had a miscarriage. I witnessed the shooting of a police officer and a carjacking and weeks later had a second miscarriage. The same week I had to be escorted through caution tape by a SWAT officer to our back door because of another shooting in our alley. Nate lost a job, gained a job, and we moved cross-country again. We sold one house and bought another and had to sell it eight months later. We lost our entire savings account and down payment. This all before even one year of marriage had passed.

This is all of what we were carrying—or rather, what we weren't carrying—when we walked into a counselor's office near our new home in Washington, DC. We weren't carrying a sense of safety or security. We weren't carrying joy or a baby. We weren't carrying ourselves upright. We barely crossed the threshold intact.

Once we were in his office, he asked why we were there, and we ticked down that same list, adding also that I was terrified of driving in a car without the doors locked, that loud noises made my body a stranger, that sex was beginning to feel like the precursor to death. We said we couldn't agree on where to go to church or even if. And then we were silent, waiting, I suppose, for some silver bullet from the mouth of this therapist. Or even something to relieve our pain.

He sat there for a minute and then took off his glasses, looked at us, and said, "You've told me what happened and what you think about what happened, but do you have any feelings about what happened? I know what you think, but what do you *feel*?"

And I suppose that might have been the first time I became cognizant of that question and its power.

Our counselor gave us a feelings wheel[1] that day, and we stuck it to our refrigerator. We began learning not to say, "I'm sad." Instead, we would say, "I feel powerless" or "I feel empty." We began learning anger was just what was visible, but beneath that anger was probably the feeling of betrayal or violation. We learned there were a lot of ingredients to a simple thing like sadness or anger or fear or even happiness, but we also might have to hunt them down and name them.

I am not from an environment that values feelings. Instead, I was taught from a young age that feelings weren't facts or feelings couldn't be trusted and that hearts were desperately wicked and also couldn't be trusted. We were taught to dry our tears quickly and to smooth things over swiftly. I learned that tears were a sign of weakness and that my own anger was anathema, even if my father's was always justified. I faced the world armed with facts and tried to think my way through everything.

The most potent pain of my life had been the death of my younger brother when I was nineteen, and I wept for a week, and perhaps a few times throughout that year. I remember five moments of tears throughout the rest of my twenties: once, when I heard my parents' divorce was finalized; once, after a horrible Christmas trying to navigate their divorce and my six siblings and an endless custody battle; once, when a boyfriend and I ended our relationship; once, when I found out a truth my parents tried to keep hidden; and once, when my car broke down in the middle of a blizzard on Christmas night four hours from home and a friend and I spent the night on hard benches in the dark McDonald's where a cop dropped us off.

Then I was dry for more than a decade.

A feelings wheel is helpful for naming a feeling, but even naming it is still just *thinking* the feeling and not feeling it.

I lied above. I didn't start saying, "I feel powerless" or "I feel empty." Instead, I would say, "I *think* I feel powerless" or "I *think* I feel empty." I couched the feeling in analysis because actually *feeling* powerless or empty would remind me that I'm mere dust and that dust is just dead particles, and I was terrified of dying. Or perhaps I was terrified of how it would actually feel to die.

At the time, I wondered if I could think my way into feeling or pray my way into it. After we began counseling, I began praying, "God, would you give me the gift of tears over the grief in my own life? Would you help me *feel* the hurt and not just think it?" Madeleine L'Engle once wrote, "I pray for courage to mourn so that I may be strengthened,"[2] and I realized that courage was what I needed more than anything. Courage to mourn what was mournful. To feel what hurt. To let it matter. To let it, in some ways, change me into something entirely new and different. To weep over what had broken.

Another ingredient the soil farmer adds to his concoction: water.

Isak Dinesen noted that the cure for anything is "salt water: sweat, tears, or the sea,"[3] but I can tell you that when you pray for the courage to mourn, when it comes it does not feel like a cure. It feels like an erosion, carving out caverns from your inner self.

What I did not expect was for it to take so long to have an answered prayer. I expected that if one wants to cry, they ought to be able to eke out a tear or two and the rest would go from there. But that didn't happen. A year passed, two years, three. I would occasionally tear up when with a friend or during the ending of a good book. One night in the ER, as an ultrasound technician moved a wand within my womb because the pain was nearly unbearable, I wept. I might have cried too when the doctor came in to tell us the pregnancy was an ectopic one with zero chance of survival, but I don't remember. I just remember the shock. And then I remember the weeks and weeks of numbness that followed.

The tears, when they finally came, felt nothing like an answered prayer. They felt like a nightmare. They came over grief and pain not for my own life but for another's. The summer after we moved back to New York, three days after the sudden death of my stepfather, our family received more terrible news. This news resulted in the arrest of a family member and had aftershocks that rippled out to the community of which they were a part, and even further out to the community of which I am a part. The pain of this circumstance left nothing untouched. Its ripples touched my own childhood pain. It flowed through old friendships and new ones. It revealed misuse of power and leadership, theology formed in isolation instead of diversity. It brought a new tenderness to me for an old situation I'd struggled for years to understand. I learned in that process that the courage to mourn is closely related to the courage to challenge injustice.

I spent a whole year crying.

I cried in grief.
I cried in pain.

I cried in regret.
I cried in anger.
I cried in forgiveness.
I cried in fear.
I cried in panic.
I cried in incredulity.

Tears are like a mirror, reflecting back what matters. When I finally began to cry, I began to see the layers of brokenness that lay within and without me.

A writing friend and I have absconded to a retreat center in our beloved Adirondacks. She drove north and I drove south and we met in the middle. Many of the lakes in New York are long and thin, stretching from north to south, bodies of water like Lake Champlain, Long Lake, the Finger Lakes, and Lake George, where we are perched now with our writing and research.

Lake George is the cleanest lake in the United States, and its locals want to keep her that way, but it is February and we are in the middle of a thaw, so wherever we walk around this retreat center mud abounds. R. H. Blyth wrote, "Mud is the most poetical thing in the world,"[4] but one has to wonder if he never loved or lost or feasted or failed, because I can think of more poetic things than mud.

A person can step gingerly around the mud where they find it, or as most of us are being taught to do, we can walk right through it. Protecting the fragile ecosystem around us is more important than having to kick off the caked mud before going inside. If we circumvent the paths and walk on the drier edges, we make the paths wider, and therefore we crush the plant life, mosses, and roots below our feet, leading to more and more erosion. If caring about the land beneath our feet is a form of love, then I suppose I can see things from Blyth's point of view.

I love the time of year when the snow recedes and the scent of mud is in the air. Someone will come inside, their nose running and their fingers chilled, and inevitably say, "It smells like spring out there," and we all know what they mean. The waning winter days smell hopeful and promising, especially when you live in a place that spends most of the winter buried under snow.

But all that snow has to go somewhere. And so as she melts, she sinks into the ground and runs down to rushing and rising creeks and then makes her way to the lakes and rivers that proliferate this land. We are coming to the time of year when the waterfalls are gorgeous and the gorges are full of sparkling and clear melted snow, and also the time of year the locals call "mud season." It is warm enough to melt the snow but not warm enough to dry the ground, and so the smell of spring we love so much stays on our boots until April.

Last week there was an earthquake along the border of Turkey and Syria. On the morning after, I read there were five thousand dead. Now, a week later, that number has climbed to nearly fifty thousand. All the news, photographs, and videos coming through are devastating. Last night I watched the rescue of a small girl whose legs were crushed and would need to be amputated. She barely cried as they removed her.

Yesterday I saw a video of how the earthquake created a canyon right in the middle of an olive grove. On either side of the new gorge are green lawns and speckled groves of trees, and there, like a fresh slice through perfect skin, is now a canyon. It is not like the canyons we know, red and blue and golden sides worn smooth by rain and wind, but someday it will be. If the earth could bleed, she would be gushing. The cut is deep and wide, full of boulders and dirt, land never seen by human eyes before.

This is sometimes how I think of pain in our lives. Even if our bodies and lives are a landscape of hurt and healed wounds, because we are humans and we live in a story as unique to us as our fingerprints or DNA, every cut is new and foreign, never before seen or experienced. The question isn't yet "How do we navigate this new landscape?" but "How does this landscape even exist?" We are not at the living-with point but at the did-this-really-happen point or is-this-really-my-life point.

In the video, three or four people stand near the edge of the new canyon, looking into it. Maybe it is the farmer, maybe it is a neighbor, maybe it is just a curious passerby.

All around them fifty thousand lives have been lost, and yet this cavernous opening in the earth is where they stand and look. And why not? Maybe it is sometimes easier to look at the pain of another than at our own pain.

I used to believe that God causes our pain, intends it, in order to shape and refine us. But this view makes God not only unkind but also pragmatic, and I no longer find that view compatible with the God I see in the Bible. I am no deist either though, believing that God created all this and us and then stepped back and brushed off his hands, leaving us to navigate the whole world and life on our own. Instead, I believe there is some beautiful synergy between God and us. He beckons, we follow. We plead, he answers. He gives, we receive. He withholds, we grab it anyway. I also believe that however awful and terrible our pain is, God redeems pain. God doesn't cause it as much as allows it, because it is his prerogative to do so, just as it is our prerogative to choose against him.

As much as it pains me to admit this too, the most life-changing moments of my life have come through the most pain. When I look over the landscape of my life, I see that the seasons of concentrated pain caused seismic shifts. I have moved over the fault lines that weakened me and been strengthened in the times of crushing. I have been bent and broken but never destroyed in the midst of it all, and that is a miracle, I see now.

My favorite writer, Madeleine L'Engle, says a similar thing and helps me not feel so alone in this view: "As I look back on fifty years of this work, I am forced to accept that my best work has been born from pain. I am forced to see that my own continuing development involves pain. It is pain and weakness and constant failures which keep me from pride and help me to grow. The power of God is to be found in weakness, but it is God's power."[5]

I love that L'Engle says, "My own continuing development involves pain." She doesn't say, "I choose pain in order to develop," or "God gives me pain to develop me." Instead, she acknowledges that pain is a part of development.

She learned to walk through the mud instead of around it.

L'Engle also says, "Like the winter fields, my heart needs the snows of Lent."[6] But I need the mud of Lent—the dirt, the soil, the tease of spring followed by the final blizzard. I need the shifting complications of good weather next to bad. (What is bad weather anyway?) I need the melt and the thaw and the hopeful heads of crocuses and daffodils pushing through the dark earth, where they have been storing up energy since last fall. I need the unpredictable earthiness of late winter and early spring because it reminds me to expect paradox and the inexplicable, and also to expect to get muddy sometimes.

This excruciating pain we were walking through as a family was coupled with the need for me to get muddy, to expose a system that had protected a person who abused for five years rather than do everything within its power to care for the victims of abuse—or, at the very least, report the abuse to the authorities.

I am not by nature an activist. I do not relish conflict or run toward chaos. It sometimes feels like most of my life has been spent running from chaos and being chased by it nonetheless. It took me a month to speak to those within the system and plead with them to confront their leaders. It took another few months for me to find the nerve to confront someone with power within the system. And when none of that resulted in an admission of wrongdoing, on a warm spring day, I sat on our porch and made the decision to tell the community what their leaders had neglected to do. It was one of the messiest choices I could have made. I knew I was holding my breath and stepping into quicksand. I knew that all the pain and hurt that had come from the pandemic and politics, all the lost and hurting relationships there, would pale in comparison to what we were going to lose by speaking up and what others would lose by our choice to speak up. And I knew that by letting the wider community know, each one of them would experience a chasm of loss too. What I predicted came true.

The landscape changed. A grove split right in two, a canyon broken open between. Some stood on the edge; some looked away; some went down into it; some called anyone who stood on the other side, formerly a neighbor, an enemy; and some tried to pull others out from the rubble. In the end, no one was unchanged.

Good soil is not just the combination of good ingredients. It is also the presence of life: worms, fungi, and other microorganisms. It is teeming with the tenuous presence of both death and life. Ashes, washed-up kelp bulbs, sand split from stone, right in with all that is very much alive. And so, in one sense, soil is a living thing too.

No living thing has only one purpose, but one of the central purposes of soil is to store carbon. Plants breathe in sunlight and carbon dioxide (which we breathe out) and transform it into carbon, which in turn helps them grow. But they also send 40 percent of that carbon down into their roots, where it feeds the microorganisms that live in the soil. In a sense, plants are keeping soil alive. And because healthy soil stores carbon safely and keeps it from filling the atmosphere, soil helps keep all living things alive.

But when plants are stripped from the landscape and the

earth is tilled and crushed by bad agricultural habits, soil that is meant to absorb water and carbon dioxide instead *releases* water and carbon dioxide. This leads to less ability of the land to withstand normal wind and water, causing expedited erosion. There are no plants above the dirt to control the slow release of water into the environment, so there is massive runoff. One conservationist says that "erosion is when soil becomes dirt."[7] In the 1930s, the rapid expansion of big farming led to tilling the soil until the life was plowed out of it. We know this era as the Dust Bowl. A Cornell University study says that soil in the United States is disappearing ten times faster than the rate at which it can be replenished. In China and India, soil is disappearing thirty to forty times faster than it can be replenished. "As a result of erosion over the past 40 years, 30 percent of the world's arable land has become unproductive."[8]

Healthy soil makes healthy plants, and healthy plants make healthy soil, and healthy plants and soil make a healthier life for all. Soil expert Ray Archuleto says, "A covered planet is a healthy planet."[9] Wendell Berry says, "Given only the health of the soil, nothing that dies is dead for very long."[10] Theologian Norman Wirzba says, "God draws near to the earth and then animates it from within."[11] The scientist, the poet, and the theologian alike attest to the necessity of good soil.

Another ingredient for the soil farmer's dirt lasagna: animate life—plants, worms, fungi, and other microorganisms.

On the southeast coast of New Zealand, on a peninsula near Christchurch, there were once old-growth forests. Sometime in the 1800s, the ancient trees were cut down and used for lumber. The resource was there for the taking, and no one could anticipate the true cost of such a loss. Soon the land was almost entirely stripped, and the rolling hills that the treeless landscape revealed began to be used for farming. Rocky and hilly, it wasn't good farmland, and the farmers fought an aggressive enemy to keep the land passably farmable: gorse.

Gorse is a scrubby, woody plant with bright yellow flowers that craves the sunlight but doesn't grow tall. Instead, it spreads wide, covering whole acres in a short period of time. In most places on earth, it is considered an invasive species.

Gorse wasn't the landowners' only enemy. Absent the old-growth trees and the root systems that held together the soil below, erosion was a concern. Farmers were fighting a battle above ground and below it, and there seemed to be no easy solution. "How can we solve these problems?" everyone asked. They would cut down the gorse, and its plenteous seeds would spread, and new gorse would grow. They would finally clear a gorse-free space, and the land would erode. They would burn acres of gorse, and fire would be the thing that made the gorse seed pods open. The peninsula was telling them something, and no one was listening.

And then a local botanist asked a different question: "What if we befriend the gorse?"

Hugh Wilson noticed that beneath the shade of the gorse, plants would spring up, tiny saplings, native grasses and ferns, but when a farmer came in to remove the gorse, they would trample or remove the saplings and other young growth too.

Wilson decided to run a five-year experiment. In September 1983, he created 1,331 six-square-meter sites on Banks Peninsula land, laid out in a grid system.[12] Over the next five years, he and other scientists surveyed the plots to see what happened when gorse was simply left alone. Locals called him crazy, but he had a dream.

Within five years, his dream began to come true.

Left alone to grow, the gorse created a scrubby and low protective canopy over the land. Their roots dug in and held the soil together, creating a flourishing ecosystem below, preventing erosion and allowing saplings and other new growth a safe place to spend their infancy. And then as the saplings grew, stretching toward the sky and sunlight, they pushed through the scrubby gorse, beginning to stand taller than the weedy shrubs that had sheltered them. As the new trees began to spread their own canopies and create a new overstory for the land, the gorse, deprived of the sunlight it so desperately needed, began to die. The flowers fell off, the seeds fell onto unlit soil, the leaves dried up, looking like dried rosemary bushes, and eventually they too fell off, leaving a sculptural mess of dried shrub and roots.

Above, the new trees were flourishing, beginning to tower above the land, and as they grew and the gorse died, their roots pushed even more deeply into the ground, preventing even more erosion and providing spaces for other native plants to grow.

Forty years after his hypothesis, Hugh Wilson is still the caretaker of the Hinewai Reserve, a vibrant, lush, green, regenerating forest that will one day, he hopes, become an old-growth forest. Hopefully by then we will all have learned from our mistakes.

I am learning to befriend my pain and hurt. I am learning to have the courage to look straight at it and ask, "Why are you here and what do you want to teach me?" I am learning not to run from it or try to cut it out but to sit with it and see what might happen when its invasiveness and limitations are simply allowed to be. What might grow beneath it? What might become of it? Will it always be there? Or someday will it stop hogging all the space in my life and begin to shrivel and shrink, having done the work I needed it to do in me?

Environmental writer Terry Tempest Williams and her husband, Brooke, once attended a public lands auction for oil and gas companies that bid for leases to drill on the land, removing the natural resources that lay within the soil and earth. With no intention of drilling, Terry bid on a piece of land as a form of nonviolent protest against drilling and the removal of fossil fuels (carbon) from the ground. The couple won about one thousand acres, which they planned to leave alone for the ten years of their lease, after which, because they hadn't drilled, the land would be up for auction again. Some might say it was an act of fools rushing in, merely prolonging the degradation of the land instead of preventing it. Later, someone told Terry, "You're married to sorrow." She responded, "No, I'm not married to sorrow, I just refuse to look away."[13]

Here is sorrow. Here is hurt. Here is pain and grief and loss and the unexpected. Now sit with it and stay. Refuse to look away. Befriend it. What is it trying to teach you? What is it saying to you? What might grow beneath it if you only let it linger and don't run from it or try to think your way through its solution?

St. Francis has been credited with saying, "Our hands imbibe like roots, so I place them on what is beautiful in the world."[14] Soil is what is beautiful in the world—hidden, dark, loamy, and life giving. Make me like a plant, I am learning to pray. Give me courage to mourn what is sad and also to press down into the soil of the life I have and feed what lies beneath, in the "dark matter of earth."[15] Help me hold what is beautiful in the world, and even though it contains unexpected ashes and terrible tears, remind me it also holds the source of life.

5

HERE IS GRIEF

FOREST LITTER

We always carry around in our body the death of Jesus, so that the life of Jesus may also be revealed in our body.

—2 Corinthians 4:10

Behold this compost! Behold it well! . . .
It gives such divine materials to men, and accepts
    such leavings from them at last.

—Walt Whitman, "This Compost"

The poet knew we could not stop for death, but it was not kindness that made death stop for us.[1] Nothing in the world stops for death except the once beating heart. Kindness has nothing to do with it.

When grief comes, it comes in waves. Wake up, brush your teeth, rock back with grief. Drink your tea, open your email, answer one, get hit with grief. Make lunch, make a snack, feel an afternoon slump coming on, but you know it's not a slump; it's grief, and it will be there until you crawl into bed's relative cocoon of safety at night. Oversleep in the morning and do it all over again.

I have known real grief from real deaths, but the grief surrounding the death of friendships or relationships or institutions is another kind of grief. It's a grief with no home. The folk singer Jason Gray has a song about his divorce called "Death without a Funeral," and this has become how I think of all these little deaths. Lied to by a leader: death with no funeral. Listening to another leader endorse politicians who lie: death without a funeral. Sitting through a meal with someone who gets all their news from one deeply partisan source: death without a funeral. Texting an old friend and never hearing back: death without a funeral. Receiving a message from another old friend saying they've decided our friendship cannot withstand our personal stance on masking or vaccines or social distancing: death without a funeral. Betrayed by someone who I thought would always be there: death without a funeral.

How does one grieve these small deaths when they come so fast and furious? How does one compartmentalize when

all the issues seem so important—so literally *life and death*—
that we cannot separate our opinions from our love? We cut
and cut and cut out, trying to protect ourselves, but in the
end we're just standing there, bleeding out and alone.

Dinner does not stop for death either, and so I make a lot of
soup these days. I put the Dutch oven on the stove and drop
in a pad of butter to brown. While it melts down, I cut up a
whole onion, maybe two, which always reminds me of Father
Robert Farrar Capon's famous chapter on the onion from
The Supper of the Lamb: "Meet it on its own terms, not on
yours."[2] Perhaps the onions want to be diced, perhaps they
want to be sliced, perhaps they will be quartered and cara-
melized, maybe just sautéed. I let the onion dictate the terms.
I have not yet decided what kind of soup tonight's will be.

When the onion has simmered down a bit, I toss in some
herbs and fresh minced garlic. This is the base of a thousand
and one meals, so the possibilities are still endless.

I open the refrigerator and dig around in the produce
drawers to find whatever vegetables are beginning to age.
Some not-quite-rubbery carrots, a bag of Brussel sprouts,
a whole stalk of celery, some leeks (hmm, that might be
interesting). I'm pretty sure there are some potatoes in the
pantry nearly growing eyes of their own. Grief makes it hard
to remember to work with what you have before it dies too.

Potato-leek soup it is.

Leeks are deceptively dirty. The soil hides between every layer, and you don't necessarily see it until you've split or sliced them. I wash them thoroughly and then dice them up. Same with the celery. I eye the almost-rubbery carrots again and decide to put them in too. What can it hurt? They go into the pot to simmer down with the rest. Then I carve out all the little eyes on the aging potatoes while still leaving most of their skin on. Once the onion, leek, garlic, and carrot mix seems sufficiently cooked, I pour in a jar of bone broth that's been keeping in the back of the refrigerator since the last time we had roast chicken. When it all comes to a quiet simmer, I put in the potatoes, making sure they are covered nicely. When everything is fork tender, I dip my immersion blender into the mixture and blend it into a smooth and creamy soup. The last ingredient to almost every soup is lemon zest, and I grate it in right at the end.

I keep scraps in a bowl on the counter. In the bowl are crushed-up eggshells, the core of an apple eaten earlier in the day, the woody stems of kale left over from a green smoothie I made for breakfast. With the carrot tops and skins, the outer layer of the leeks, the butt of the celery, and the eyes of the red potatoes, it is a rainbow of color in there.

Later, after we have eaten, Nate will carry the bowl out to our makeshift compost bin, which is really just a big cardboard box we had left after our move that we've been filling with lawn clippings, leaves, and produce scraps. It is a pitiful excuse for a compost bin, but one day, I promise myself, we will do better.

In late winter, all I want to do is watch my only celebrity crush on television: Monty Don, Britain's premier gardener and host of *Gardener's World* on the BBC. His wild hair and patched linen pants and aged chore coat—this is the way to my heart. Even better if there are crocuses and hellebores, which, this time of the year, there always are.

I have never thought of myself as a gardener. When I was small and being taught that the government was a threat and the truant officers would get us if we left the house during the day and I was too shy for stores anyway, my mother found solace in her gardens. We had acres of them on our land in Bucks County, Pennsylvania. A rock garden in our backyard, boulders interspersed with bountiful perennials. Shade-loving shrubby corners by our brick walkway. And a giant vegetable garden to the south of our house.

I hated the vegetable garden. To me it was a place ripe with weeds and a demand for chores. It was also a reminder that the dream of self-sufficiency and homesteading—which I thought of as total erasure of our lives—was alive in my parents' hearts. We all took turns in the garden.

In the fall, during harvest time, my mother would pick and pickle, can and preserve, jam and water bathe until we had rows and rows of Mason jars all full of winter gold. I didn't mind the garden then.

Now, having reached the age my mother was then, I pile up my gardening books and page through them all through the last weeks of winter. I cannot wait to sink my hands into the soil and spread compost and manure over the land beneath our feet. I will invariably plant something too early, spread some seeds out prematurely, buy a plant that won't last a night outside yet. I will check on our compost bin incessantly, waiting for it to warm up, which will speed the process of breaking down its contents and signal all the microorganisms to wake up. Another British television host calls compost "brown gold," and I don't know a single gardener who disagrees.

As the snow recedes, I take to the paths again. We like snowshoeing in the winter, but I will always prefer an earthy hike on dry land. Leaves that were brilliant last fall are curled now and brittle, crunching beneath my feet. Pine needles that were malleable in autumn are now breakable, like a spaghetti strand. Ferns that unfurled last spring are now flattened to the ground like pressed botanical prints. Sticks that couldn't withstand the heavy snow and fell are hiding in the layers of brown. Ecologists and soil scientists call all of this "forest litter."

There is dampness in the air. Not one that comes down from above like rain but one that rises up from the earth below, where the moisture is, right now, helping to transform these leftovers from their former state into something almost unrecognizable. A composted state where no one will be able to tell where fern ended and leaf began. This is nature's mulch, and like the gardener's brown gold, last year's mulch is this year's soil.

C. S. Lewis, in his book on grief, writes, "Reality never repeats. The exact same thing is never taken away and given back."[3] And the same is true with all these leaves and needles and flattened plants. We will never have those same bits and pieces again. They will become something else entirely and then begin feeding the genesis of their descendants.

The decomposition of forest litter gives the soil it feeds structure and shape. A piece of bark will decompose slower than a brittle leaf, leaving a space between the two for worms and water and air to move through. Pine needles will break down even more slowly. As the water, worms, and air move through the earth, they churn it and move it, tumbling it over itself. Nothing is left untouched by the process of decomposition. Every piece of it is changed into something new.

In the throes of grief, it is easy to think the only thing that will make it better is to have the grieved-over thing back again, whole and unmarred. But I have been through grief enough times to know that on the eventual other side there is a different kind of whole. I will never call death good, but I think I could call grief good. The process of grief is learning to live without the thing that has been taken away. It is learning to live in subtraction. Even if another good is added eventually, what was subtracted is never added in again. The former life has gone. There is a new normal now.

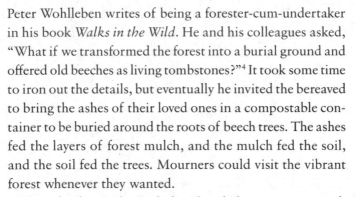

Peter Wohlleben writes of being a forester-cum-undertaker in his book *Walks in the Wild*. He and his colleagues asked, "What if we transformed the forest into a burial ground and offered old beeches as living tombstones?"[4] It took some time to iron out the details, but eventually he invited the bereaved to bring the ashes of their loved ones in a compostable container to be buried around the roots of beech trees. The ashes fed the layers of forest mulch, and the mulch fed the soil, and the soil fed the trees. Mourners could visit the vibrant forest whenever they wanted.

Some leaders in the Catholic Church, however, protested. Because of their belief in the sacredness of the human body, they worried that because the composting ashes would turn into other matter—namely, roots and trees—this would prevent the rising of the physical body in the coming kingdom of God. But even sacred things become, as John Keating in the movie *Dead Poet's Society* reminds his students, "food for worms, lads."

In the south of Seattle, on the banks of the Duwamish Waterway, there is an ivy-covered building full of rotting human bodies. This is no mortuary, nor is it the haunt of a serial killer. It is one of the first human decomposition facilities in the United States.[5]

When a person dies and is buried with traditional methods, they are filled with embalming chemicals, housed in a casket that is then encased in concrete, and then buried in the earth. This process prevents—or at least slows—the process of decomposition. As time goes on though, available land for graveyards is becoming scarce, and within the past seventy years, there has been a new demand for cremation. Now almost 50 percent of people choose to be cremated. But the cremation process uses an incredible amount of energy, deposits ash into the atmosphere, and pollutes the air with more than six hundred million pounds of carbon dioxide. While in graduate school, New England native Katrina Spade realized that "the very last thing we do on earth is poison it"[6] and decided to explore other avenues for the care of dead bodies.

What she found was a process called Livestock Mortality Composting, which farmers had been using to dispose of dead cattle. Essentially, the farmers would take the nitrogen-rich body of a dead cow and cover it over with carbon-rich material. With natural breezes and rainwater, it would take

about nine months for the body to completely decompose—
bones, flesh, everything.

"Why can't we," Spade asked, "use a similar process for
humans?"[7]

She began to research the best and most ethical way of
letting the last thing bodies do on earth become the feeding
of it instead of the thieving from it. Spade founded Recompose in the winter of 2020 after more than seven years of
research, studies, and fundraising.

The process may seem complex, but it is simple. Inside the
Recompose facility is a vertical container filled with plant
matter like wood chips and other carbon-rich material. The
family of mourners holds a small funeral ceremony, and then
the body of their loved one is lowered into the container and
covered over with more plant matter. As the body decom-
poses, it turns into carbon-rich material, and then when the
body has been completely broken down, the soil is brought
to Bell Mountain, a local reserve near Seattle, where it will
regeneratively feed the forest. Washington State was the first
state in the US to approve human composting, but since
then five more states have passed laws allowing it: Colorado,
Oregon, Vermont, California, and, as of a few weeks ago,
my own state, New York.

"In nature," Spade says, "death creates life."[8]

The decomposition of our bodies is an uncomfortable
truth, as is most of grief. Our rational minds know that the
body before us is not fully the person we knew and loved

and were known and loved by. Human life is sacred, and we cannot let go of what once lived quite so quickly. The same goes for lost friendships and relationships. As grief begins to touch every part of our new life, moving through us, churning us up, we will never be the same again. How could we be?

I once watched a time-lapse video of the composting process. It took ten minutes to watch sixty days of worms turning food scraps, leaves, sticks, and other matter into rich, dark, loamy soil. Rebecca Solnit writes, "In order to see change you have to be slower than it,"[9] and I believe that's true for grief too. If we want assurance that something good is being worked in us during our grief, we could speed up the process, like the time-lapse video. But grief slows us down instead. We walk as though weighed down with the world and worry and wonder of what no longer is. Checking the mailbox takes Herculean effort. Answering a friend's phone call is exhausting. Making dinner feels impossible. Life seems to unfold in slow motion, while all around us the world just keeps moving on.

Just as death fundamentally changes the one who has died, grief fundamentally changes the griever. We could pretend it doesn't, but that wouldn't work for long.

The intentional breaking down of the body—as opposed to preserving it through traditional burial methods—is not without controversy. Every week when I say the Apostles' Creed with my church family, I say the words "I believe . . . in the resurrection of the body." How can I believe in the resurrection of something that no longer exists as flesh? Again, I'm reminded of N. T. Wright's words, "God can do new things with dust."[10] God scooped dust from the earth once and created man, and I have to believe he can scoop soil from a forest and remake the same man again. St. Paul wrote to the Corinthians, "The body that is sown is perishable, it is raised imperishable" (1 Cor. 15:42).

Nothing smells as good as a handful of mulched earth. Food writer and journalist Michael Pollan writes of compost, "If fertility has a perfume, this surely was it."[11] I had a friend in the Texas suburbs once who hated to be outside because she didn't like the way she smelled when she came inside. I didn't understand this until I began to pay attention to it myself. She was right. Where we lived smelled of hot concrete and dust, rubber, and exhaust from vehicles. Whenever I would visit home in the North, one of the things I'd look forward to most was the scent. Sometimes I'd be driving back to Upstate New York, and I'd pull the car over on a quiet stretch still an hour from home. I would get out and stand on the side of the road and breathe in balsam and woodsmoke and fresh, clean, clear air. These are things we take for granted in some places, or things we can't imagine existing in other places.

I told my friend that if she ever visited me here, she'd love the smell of being outside. Years later, she visited the Pacific Northwest, and after she got home she told me, "You were right, Lo, the smell of the outdoors was so beautiful it made me cry."

The smell is earth. The scent is life.

But it carries with it the fragrance of death.

How can something decaying still smell so alive?

Try it. Stand in the woods or a garden or the landscape section of a big-box store and scoop a handful of earth into your hands. This earth was once bright green leaves and tree bark and animal excrement and mosses and fungi. It is the great composition of life and a symphony of death. It is a paradox. Robin Wall Kimmerer writes, "We have to put our hands in the earth to make ourselves whole again."[12]

And so too with grief. We have to engage it as it is, hold it as it is, let it hold us as we are, and as we do, sorrow will help us find the way through to a wholeness again.

Here is a confession, reader. I don't know how to write this part of this story. Grief disorients us, and it can be hard to tell where your pain ends and another's begins, or where yours starts and another's ends. It is also difficult to tell a story that is not only yours or not primarily yours to tell. One runs into the problem of being too vague or too specific. And without being able to share the specifics of a story, a person runs the risk of seeming narcissistic, as if all the pain is about them. I am only a fraction of those who have been touched by the grief I am writing of, and yet that fraction matters too. My work is not to ask you to look at my grief and think of me but to show you a grief so common you can face your own.

Sometimes a writer must ask a reader to simply trust them as they lead them down a sometimes-dark path. Poet David Whyte says that in times of darkness we must sometimes go toward the darkness because that is where we will find we are not beyond love.[13] Part of grief is being able to hold the grief of others without always knowing why or how. Sometimes in our darkest moment, we will sit beside another who is in an even darker moment, and here we will be tested: Is there room in the cavern in me for the cavern in you too?

Just as I struggle to cry, I struggle, too, to grieve. Grieving conflicts with my desire for peace and an absence of interruption. I do not want to give the attention grief demands. Poet John O'Donohue writes, "Sorrow will remain faithful to itself. More than you, it knows its way,"[14] and I am still learning the truth of this. To grieve is an act of trust, an act of faith. Some might say it is faith or trust in God, but I've been there before, and I know that in the throes of grief, God often feels far away. Instead, I have to put some faith in the sorrow, trusting it will work its way through me and bring me to a new or different place in the end. It will change my capacity to grieve with others. It will alter my ability to hold another's mourning. It will enlarge the space within me that holds empathy and sympathy.

In a potent moment of grief over all that was falling apart around me, I felt a blinding anger rise within me. I have spent most of my life convincing myself and others that I am not an angry person. But in more recent years, I have begun to realize that beneath the still waters of my personality is a strong undercurrent of anger. I felt anger at injustice, anger at people who lied, anger at the strong belittling the weak. I was angry at being misrepresented, angry at the news, angry with people who tried to get me to express my anger by baiting me to fight with them.

I grew up with an angry father who would shout and throw things, who struck holes in our walls and who seethed when crossed. I learned to cower from his anger, but sometimes when I felt brave enough, I would say, "Please stop yelling."

"This isn't yelling," he would yell. And then he would raise his voice even more. "If you want me to yell," he would pause here for effect, "this is me yelling!" and his voice would reverberate through my body.

And so I learned to mistrust the anger of others, to assume my estimation of their anger was always wrong. And

I learned to distrust my own anger, afraid it would turn me into someone like my father, who wouldn't admit the power of his own voice. What I didn't realize, though, is that by pretending I didn't feel anger, I was not admitting the power of my own voice or the emotion I had toward the thing I was angry about.

As we moved into the second year of the pandemic and more racial conflicts, the events of January 6 and the ensuing breakdown of relationships, the grief our family was feeling about the loss of our grandmother and stepfather and the details surrounding a family member's arrest for abuse, it felt like there was so much to be angry about but no one person to be angry with. There was loss everywhere but no one person with whom to make peace.

I listened to a popular podcast at the time about the implosion of a church in Seattle and thought, *There's so much hurt in the world, and no one person can make it better*. No one person had the solution or resolution for what was breaking apart. If a church asked people to wear masks, a whole swath of people would leave. If a church didn't ask folks to wear masks, another swath of people would leave. If a church supported the police, people would leave. If a church talked about systemic racism, people would leave. And so on. Each group would say, "Good riddance," feeling morally superior to the other group. The fractures in our society were on full display, and it seemed like we would never be whole again.

We all wanted a handbook for how to navigate this time in history, but there was none. Mental health crises were on the rise, loneliness was epidemic, violence was beginning to erupt everywhere. Inflation was rising and unemployment was too. Housing prices were astronomical and so was rent. The more internal and external pressures we all faced, the less capable we felt of knowing what was best in any situation. Everything just felt messy and muddy and mixed up, with no space to breathe or weep before the next crushing blow. It was a thousand deaths without funerals.

In most deciduous forests, there are three layers to the forest floor before you get down to soil. The top layer is forest litter: leaves, sticks, bark, and needles—carbon-rich plant matter through which the air breezes and blows. One ecologist calls forest litter "the capillary system of the forest, removing waste and conveying food to the legions of consumers below."[15] The "consumers" below break down that plant matter to form what scientists call the fermented horizon. This layer traps the moisture from the air and rain. Below this layer is the humic horizon, where the plant matter is almost unrecognizable now. It has broken down almost completely, and mycelia (fungi) are beginning to turn it into the dark, rich layers of soil below. If you went to a deciduous forest right now, you could peel back these three layers like a carpet and see each of them clearly.

In order to complete the decomposition process and become nutrient-rich, loamy soil, the compost needs air, water, and other microorganisms. And likewise with us. In order to heal, we need space to breathe, permission to weep, and the presence of a friend who will help us make sense of it all: air, water, and living things. Or as Diane Langberg says, "Trauma healing always requires talking, tears, and time."[16]

But what do you do when it all happens too fast, too close, too alone? I had nowhere to put my lament and grief. Like my anger, it just churned deep within me.

I realized I was waiting for the funeral before I would acknowledge all these deaths, and this is no way to live. I needed the finality of standing over a grave, of scooping up a handful of dirt and letting it fall over the coffin in order to believe these relationships and institutions and communities were never going to be alive in the same way again. Until I could stop for death, sit with death, stay with death, acknowledge its presence, and let what had existed before simply now go to rest, I was going to keep feeling guilty for being unable to save a lifeless corpse.

How do you know when to walk away from the grave?

How do you wake up no longer hoping it was a bad dream?

I needed a funeral, a ritual or rite. A way to lay to rest all that was lost these past few years and all that would never be the same again.

Around this time, I heard theologian Dru Johnson speak about Christian rituals. I am still new to the practice of liturgy in the church, having spent less than a decade in the Anglican tradition, and so Christian *rituals* can still sound like magical thinking or, worse, pagan thinking. But Johnson says, "We theologize through performance."[17] In other words, whether we like it or not, how we act says what we believe to be true. Pretending I didn't feel anger was only betraying my fear of *acting* angry; it was not the absence of anger within me. Pretending dead things could still be revived was only revealing my misplaced hope.

I cannot just sit with my grief and ask it to teach me something. I must be willing for it to make me into something new, to reform and reorder me at a cellular level, to change what is perishable into something imperishable. I must be willing to act my grief, not just feel it. I needed a funeral, even if I held it alone.

I dug into a box of old fabric supplies, found a mess of colored embroidery thread and a small hoop. I fit a piece of plain, cheap muslin into the hoop and began untangling colors from the pile, choosing at random.

Blue for my grief over politics and the loss of relationships it had brought.

Red for my grief over the pandemic and our losses to it.

Green for the loss of my church family and for the breakdown of the church over these years.

Yellow for the loss of a friendship.

Purple for the ways I'd failed my Black brothers and sisters.
Orange for the Capitol insurrection.
Fuchsia for the division and grief in my family.
Gray for the stolen innocence of those I loved.
Pink for the fear I felt showing up in a friendship.
Black for the theology I was beginning to doubt.
White for the worry that I'd never feel like myself again.

I began to stitch the colors across the circle, each color intertwined with another like a rope, until I reached the middle of the hoop, and there I stitched a frayed end, as though the rope had broken from the tension. As I pushed the needle down through the fabric and pulled it back up, as I threaded a new color and another one, as I intertwined them with one another, I prayed and I confessed and I wept and I acknowledged my anger and grief. I let the dead things die.

Across from the frayed colored ends, I began another frayed end and stitched the other side of the rope to the other edge. It wasn't on purpose, but the new side of rope was made of rich, deep, loamy brown-gold thread.

6

HERE IS TIME

LICHEN

For we who are alive are always being given over to death for Jesus' sake, so that his life may also be revealed in our mortal body.

—2 Corinthians 4:11

Men have not language to describe one moment
of your eternal life.

—Ralph Waldo Emerson, "Woods"

Across the river from our house is a community graveyard sprawling under canopies of coniferous and deciduous trees. It is on a peninsula surrounded on three sides by the river, with shallow marshes to the south, swift-flowing water to the east, and a wide-open expanse to the north. The paths around and through it are carpeted by pine needles, soft for the walker or the mourner. More than a thousand bodies have been laid to rest in the cemetery, some as recently as last week, others there since the Revolutionary War. Some of the tombstones are so old that they are slowly being eaten away by crawling green lichen, and it is difficult to tell who lies beneath or for how long they have been there.

No one plants lichen; lichen isn't even a plant. Robin Wall Kimmerer says that lichen "volunteers to put down roots and homestead stone, metaphorically of course, since they have no roots."[1] Lichen is likely to be everywhere. It hunts for the route of least resistance and flourishes when left alone. Some lichens grow so slowly that it can take them a hundred years to become as big as the palm of your hand. Most of us walk past two-hundred-year-old relics in the forest without seeing them at all. They hide in plain sight. The oldest lichen known to us is nearly nine thousand years old.[2] D. W. Winnicott once wrote, "It is a joy to be hidden and a disaster not to be found."[3] And this seems apropos of the life of lichen.

Once a friend and I were hiking, and she kept stopping to put her nose right up against a tree trunk. I wondered what she was doing, but out of respect for all the odds things we do while hiking, I didn't ask. Finally, around the fifth or sixth tree, she exclaimed loudly, "I found it!"

"It" was *Lobaria pulmonaria*, a lettuce-like lichen clinging to the side of a giant spruce tree.

"Why did you want to find it?" I asked.

"No reason," she said. "I just wanted to." She ran her fingers lightly over the edges of the fungi and then, as is her nature, continued down the trail. Merlin Sheldrake, the author of the acclaimed *Entangled Life*, writes that "nature is an event that never stops."[4] So too with my friend.

Nate and I have been working slowly through a Netflix series called *Chef's Table*, and last night we watched an episode called "Jeong Kwan." If you're unfamiliar with *Chef's Table*, its fare is to craft a story from the life and work of famous chefs. Most of them work at Michelin star kitchens as world-renowned food artists.

This particular episode, though, is about the life of a Buddhist nun named Jeong Kwan. Jeong Kwan has lived and worked at a monastery in South Korea for fifty years and has no Michelin stars or cookbooks to her name. The recipients of her food artistry are her fellow nuns and novices and very occasionally visitors to the cloister.

She works in relative secret.

Unlike me, she does not use onions or garlic or leeks as the base of a thousand dishes.

Her main ingredient, one critic says, is time.[5]

Traditional soy sauce is made by fermenting soy and wheat berries using airborne or added fungi (yeast or mold or both). The kind of soy sauce we buy off the grocery store shelf has been rapidly produced in usually under a year, but Jeong Kwan uses a starter that has been passed down for generations, each batch fermented with fungi that has grown for a hundred years or more. Jeong Kwan ferments vegetables long past a normal fermentation process, leaving cabbage or other vegetables mixed with salt in giant clay jars for years. After tasting some of Jeong Kwan's food, a *New York Times* writer said, "Here were flavors so assertive they seemed to leave vapor trails on the tongue."[6]

Jeong Kwan plates the meals she serves her sister monks with as much care as the meals she serves to Michelin star chefs who come to visit their monastery. One chef says, "Jeong Kwan has no ego," and she herself says, "Creativity and ego cannot go together. If you free yourself from the competing and jealous mind, your creativity opens up endlessly. Just as water springs from a fountain, creativity springs from every moment. You must not be your own obstacle. You must not be owned by the environment you're in."[7] Working with food, it seems, is an act of worship for her.[8] Time, it seems, is no concern of hers.

For over a hundred years, lichen has been known to be, as one poet writes, a "marriage of fungi and algae, chemists of air."[9]

Sometimes even a marriage of three. I looked up *Lobaria pulmonaria* after my hike and found that the third organism in its symbiotic relationship is cyanobacterium. Merlin Sheldrake writes of the discovery of this organism in 1867 by a Swiss botanist named Simon Schwendener. "Schwendener's suggestion was vehemently opposed by his fellow lichenologists. The idea that three different species could come together in the building of a new organism with its own separate identity was shocking to many."[10] Later, Schwendener was proven right. As unlikely as it seems, these separate organisms came together and made a new organism.

One might think such a miracle would be rare, but lichen is everywhere in the forest, on every tree and rock and branch. Lichen is thought to be the "largest single system [for nitrogen fixation] in an old-growth forest."[11] This strange amalgam of three is, literally, keeping the trees alive. If you take a brief rest midway through a hike to sit down on a nearby boulder, when you stand up and keep walking, you will carry lichen spores with you, and they will scatter, finding new rocks and trees to adopt as their homes. They will lose a part of themselves and find new communities. They will carry microorganisms and markers from their former homes and knit them into a new life.

Some fungi stay airborne, which is how we get sourdough bread and soy sauce, kombucha and kimchi, yogurt and beer.

In the early days of the pandemic, everyone everywhere seemed to be making sourdough bread, and having never tried making it myself, I bought the sourdough bible everyone recommended and sent Nate out to the store to get the last remaining bag of flour on the shelves.

I labeled a Mason jar STARTER and diligently took out and added the appropriate amounts of the flour and water mix every day, leaving the lid slightly lifted—better to catch the airborne yeast. I bought a dough scraper. I read about crumb—the air pockets that form in the dough as it rises. I read a hundred different ways to perfect the crumb. And finally I placed the soft and neat round in my Dutch oven and waited for the end result.

I couldn't seem to perfect my loaf. The loaves I made were good, but never good enough. They had crumb, but never enough. They rose nicely, but they lost the perfect cuts I'd razored through them to prevent them from splitting. They were soft, but they lacked the sharpness that one expects from a loaf of sourdough. We slathered slices with butter or jam or compote, dipped them into hearty soups, or grilled them with cheeses and fruits, but after a few weeks, I gave up on sourdough.

Later, I read that the more you make sourdough in one place, the better the sourdough becomes. Why? Because of the airborne yeast and how it continues to transform over time. One baker has had the same starter in a jar in his bakery since his father opened the bakery decades ago, and his bread is renowned for its flavor. Time is its essential ingredient, making it better and better and better.

What happens, though, when time seems to be taking too long?

A Wendell Berry quotation from *The Art of the Commonplace* gives shape to my time back in this place: "And so here, in the place I love more than any other and where I have chosen among all other places to live my life, I am more painfully divided within myself than I could be in any other place."[12]

Wendell is my teacher and probably the one I have learned more from than any other writer. It helps to read those words and remember that someone who seems to me so perfectly settled and grounded in every sense of the word still felt painfully divided within himself.

I feel it too.

In coming home here during the pandemic and the fraught election year and then facing an unimaginable grief with a myriad of effects, I must make peace with the reality that no matter how much time passes, some things will never be resurrected. And it's not just here either. Almost no organization or institution or community I've been a part of in recent years has remained as it was. Some things will never be the same again. I feel like I keep groping in the dark, trying to find my way back to the place where people accepted one another and their differences without erasing one another from their lives. Back to the place where differences were part of what made a community alive and growing and transforming. I keep thinking, *If I do this or they do that, perhaps we can find our way back*. But the question I always find myself pausing on this: Why would I want to go back?

Until my midthirties or so, I had a hierarchy in my heart that gave the most sway to whichever man was at the top. I looked to these men for guidance, direction, hope, belief. I was taught there was beauty in submitting to them and that my role as a female was to joyfully put myself under their thumb and headship, listening to them and obeying whatever they thought was best for my life.

I finally extricated myself from environments where this was the norm, and it has taken me years to untangle the membranes of how this belief has shaped me. It was stuck to everything—my work, my relationships, my belief in God, my politics, my friendships, my schooling, and more. I didn't realize how absolutely terrified I was to disagree. To dissent meant to meet with disapproval and disdain and to being outcast, and this was my terror. I sought permission for everything.

I was so afraid of dissent in my early twenties that when my mother left my father, I sided with those who excommunicated her, those who slandered her new partner, and those who testified against her. I was so afraid of losing the tenuous relationships in my life that I barely spoke to her for more than a decade.

I'm not proud of this. I know I was acting out of self-protection and fear. I regret it and wish, almost more than anything, I could go back to that girl and love her into making a different choice.

The tension I feel these days, though, is that I have loved so many people who believe all those same things still, and those people believe I am sinful for the freedom I live in. Someone I love who is still in that environment says she's afraid of where this freedom leads and hopes I will repent. Repentance means "to turn and go the other way." If that is what she means, then I will never repent. For me, to repent was to turn and go the other way from them, and there I found hope and life in Jesus that weren't tied to how a person viewed gender roles or how they voted or how they educated their children or whether they took medicine for their depression. But I also found beauty in complexity. I began to learn that unity doesn't mean uniformity and that different kinds of people can commune with one another, even amid deep disagreement.

Can repentance ever mean to keep on walking until you find your way through, even if the future is unknown?

Sheldrake writes about what he calls "living labyrinths," saying, "Imagine if you could pass through two doors at once. It's inconceivable, yet fungi do it all the time. When faced with a forked path, fungal hyphae don't have to choose one or the other. They can branch and take both routes."

He goes on, "One can confront hyphae with microscopic labyrinths and watch how they nose their way around. If obstructed, they branch. After diverting themselves around an obstacle, the hyphen tips recover the original direction of their growth."[13]

Sheldrake likens the fungi's problem-solving to the way humans make their way through IKEA. There's mainly one way to move through the store—the way the long and winding aisle takes us. But there are surprising shortcuts along the way if we'll notice them—a sudden split between the rows of throw pillows, a glimpse of dining room furniture from the bedroom displays, the reflection of mirrors through a doorway in the lighting section. "They [fungi] find the shortest path to the exit,"[14] he writes. This would be like my entering our nearest IKEA, in Ottawa, Canada, and starting at the beginning of that long aisle and finding the quickest way downstairs past the cashiers to the cinnamon rolls. Not exactly but similarly. The fungi's main job is to fill the environment with itself, and it's going to take the fastest and easiest route to get there—even if it takes an eternity.

I can be my own worst enemy. I know I've been writing about the sudden and unfamiliar feeling of becoming someone's enemy because of how I voted or what I thought was a reasonable response to a pandemic or my position on reporting abuse to the proper authorities, but the truth is I talk myself out of more than half of what occurs to me, including things that are really, truly good for me and others. I have to talk myself into decisive action on almost everything, restricting my options until there is no other choice. I do not trust my first or second inclination on almost anything and am always able to see the other side with clarity and exactitude. I "on the other hand" just about everything to an almost obsessive degree.

It has taken me a long time—too long, some might say—to learn to hear the quiet voice within me and to trust it. Some might call the voice their gut or intuition, others might call it their spirit or the Holy Spirit, and still others might just think of it as common sense or their heart's desire. For me, that voice has always been dull, not even a whisper. I don't know when I learned to distrust the sound and tenor of it, but a verse from the Bible that says how desperately wicked and untrustworthy one's heart is probably had something to do with it.

In the absence (or the stifling) of this common sense or intuition or gut or Spirit's leading, I learned to look outside myself for direction. I looked to men who postured themselves as leaders and heads, to women who called themselves mentors and mothers. I looked to my peers whose lives seemed served up on silver platters. I looked behind me, at the writers I admired, and ahead of me, at the people I wanted to become like. I leaned on institutions and my environments to give me meaning or standing. I struggled to know what I believed and so looked around me to see what others believed and espoused that. And because I was never courageous enough to look within, I was never courageous enough to see my only source of strength in life was Christ alone within me.

One of those writers I admired wrote, "The place God calls you to is the place where your deep gladness and the world's deep hunger meet."[15] It would be years before I would be able to marry my delight with the world's hunger, and I'm still not sure I do it most of the time—but I know what it *feels* like to feel in the center of goodness, on the road to beautiful. It is like resonance instead of dissonance, peace instead of a twist in my gut, deep knowing instead of deep doubt.

Another poet, Denise Levertov, writes about being like a dog, "intently haphazard," and this is how I am learning to move through life. The dog, she writes, stays in motion, "changing pace and approach but not direction," then she finishes with a quote from Rilke, "every step an arrival."[16]

I typed out words from a psalm and tacked them to our kitchen wall: "The boundary lines have fallen for me in pleasant places; surely I have a delightful inheritance. I will praise the LORD, who counsels me; even at night my heart instructs me. I keep my eyes always on the LORD. With him at my right hand, I will not be shaken" (Ps. 16:6–8). This has become a promise to me of sorts, that even when I am asleep to my heart, God is still counseling and directing me. God has not abdicated my innermost being. He has put down roots and abides there, and therefore my gut or intuition or sense or spirit *is* trustworthy, even if I don't know where I'm being led or if I'll get there in one piece. I am learning, though, to be very quiet and to, in more of Oliver's words, let "things take the time they take."[17] I know I will get there eventually.

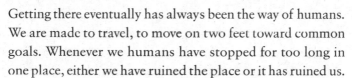

Getting there eventually has always been the way of humans. We are made to travel, to move on two feet toward common goals. Whenever we humans have stopped for too long in one place, either we have ruined the place or it has ruined us.

In nearly all religious traditions of the world, there have been pilgrims making pilgrimages to less-than-common places. Muslims to Mecca, Roman Catholics to the Vatican, Buddhists to Lumbini, and Jews to the Western Wall. As I write this, I am planning to take a group of pilgrims to Israel, where we will walk the streets of Galilee and Jerusalem, eat with Palestinian Christians, and share communion in the Garden of Gethsemane.

Thousands of years before Christ, humans began using an image of a labyrinth as an illustration of a journey. No one knows exactly when it was first used or why, though a labyrinthine image shows up in Greek mythology and on Grecian coins around 400 BC. A thousand years ago, the round Chartres labyrinth began being constructed on the floors of cathedrals and in gardens of the wealthy, the most famous inlaid on the floor of the Notre Dame Cathedral in Paris. Worshipers can walk the forty-foot-wide intricate pattern to the flower shape in the center, roughly 850 feet in length. There is only one path in and out.

It is said that Christians adopted the labyrinth as a sort of pilgrimage for those who could not make a journey elsewhere. Pilgrims and parishioners could bring their cares and concerns, fears and anxieties to the labyrinth and practice giving them to the Lord while they walked. Unlike with a maze, there are no shortcuts or multiple ways of going. There is only one way, and it is around and around until you come to the center. Yet the path weaves in and out and back and forth around itself in a pattern that reveals that none of our journeys move in a linear fashion. There are always forward and backward, upward and downward in this life.

The first day of spring is in two days, and there is again a layer of snow of varying heights covering our geographic area. Somehow, though, it feels better to leave the two inches of snow and 46 degrees at home and go to where there are two feet of snow and it is 39 degrees.

I drive south to an area of the Adirondacks I rarely venture to. The best waterways and mountains are due east of us. South of us are complex bogs and winding rivers and rapids, acres of deep wilderness and old growth. In the year I was born, the Olympics were held in the Adirondacks—the year of the Miracle on Ice, when the Russians and Americans went head-to-head on the hockey rink—and Lake Placid is still home to an Olympic training center and athletes from around the world. I drive south on the Olympic Trail Scenic Byway, which is usually beautiful but right now is edged by three feet of snow on either side. In December I would have said even that was beautiful, but in March all I want to see is green.

My destination is Wanakena, on the shores of Cranberry Lake, a lakeside hamlet that services mostly summer residents, through-hikers, and the nearby forestry school. I have heard there is a labyrinth there. I wanted to wait until the snow melted, but who has time for that anymore? I've zoomed in on the satellite map on my phone, and I can see right where it is, a Santa Rosa labyrinth, right on the edge of town, formed on a peaceful green knoll. Even with the snow, there should still be the relative shape of the edges, enough for me to walk through with my snowshoes strapped on.

One of the more famous labyrinths—before, as with many things Christians borrowed from pagans, the church adopted their use in places of worship—is from the Greek myth of King Minos of Crete keeping his monster stepson, Minotaur, in a labyrinth. As time went on, the center of the labyrinth became known as a place to hold evil spirits. Eventually, the evil spirits became vices, burdens, or sins the Christian needed to off-load or physically give to God. I don't know what I need to off-load or give to God today, but I've never walked a prayer labyrinth before, and I want to.

I park my car at a small general store called Otto's Abode and go in to ask the proprietor the best way to experience Wanakena in March. He beams with pride, and I know it's pride because I've seen his weekly missives online, which include a flurry of snapshots from around town and a run-on paragraph of all the little happenings, posted every single Thursday without fail. He tells me about the historic footbridge, shattered by an ice jam a few years back and just freshly rebuilt. He mentions the nearby cafe and recommends a sandwich I should try. I tell him I'm curious about the labyrinth, and he says, "Oh yes! It is covered with snow now, but you should be able to walk it if you have snowshoes." I do, I tell him, and he nods approvingly. I say thank you and ask if I may leave my car parked out front. "Yes, yes," he says. "Enjoy yourself."

I pull my snowshoes out of my car, strap them on my back, and walk down to the footbridge. It's an engineering feat, the locals say, the first of its kind.

I want to make the loss of relationships and the crumbling of institutions all their fault and not mine. Their isolationism, their idolatry, their idealism about what constitutes faithfulness. But the truth is it takes two to drift apart through time or willfulness. One leaves or the other lets them or both leave. It's never all down to one of us.

"You've changed," an old friend levels at me on a hot summer night, and I reply, "Of course I have." I'm forty, not twenty. I'm wise, not naive. I'm scarred, not fresh. I'm sure, not unsure. "I am still changing," I say back, and God help me to always be.

It rankles me that I am expected to be unchanged, still weak and unsure, still easily folded by conflict or disapproval, still intimidated by whispers behind my back. Someone says I have reinvented myself, crafted a story about myself that doesn't match their recollection of me from fifteen years ago. I wonder to myself, *Do you have a microscope, an X-ray, a molecular view? Do you have perfect insight into the morphing and malleability of a person, how one grows by degrees or changes over time? No? Then why is my change, my slow migration from there to here so threatening to you? Aren't we all crafting our story as we go? Snipping here and shaping there, shaving off here and sifting there, until we finally find ourselves? Oh. There I am. Ecce adsum.*

If I can find my way to my own self through all this time, perhaps we can find our way to a new way of being together, I think to myself.

129

There is still a foot of snow covering the labyrinth, but the locals have placed a series of bamboo garden poles meant to help "guide" the walker through the path. I put "guide" in quotation marks because the poles are nothing more than markers for where to stop and start. One must have traversed this circuit before in order to make sense of their spacing.

I strap on my snowshoes and stand at the entrance, realizing I haven't given much thought to this experience. Is walking a labyrinth like walking through most of life, not really knowing what it will look like until you're well on your way? Or should I, like the saints of old, come with intention and plan?

To the naked eye, lichen have neither intention nor plan. They will use almost anything to gain advantage and cover ground. It is thought that over 8 percent of the earth's surface is covered in lichen, more than twenty thousand varieties. How are they so prolific?

They find unity within diversity. They meld with a completely different species and make their way through. When one lacks the nutrients needed for survival, the other compensates, and vice versa. To flourish, lichen has to work within its own complex yet symbiotic relationship. "By vanishing in it," Berry writes in one poem, "becoming what he never was."[18] Can these disparate parts vanish into a whole new thing, becoming some entirely new? Is it possible?

"God, make me more like lichen," I whisper as I lift my poles and begin to create my own path through the snow. I get halfway around and my geometry is terrible. Wavering lines of steps weave in and out, looking like there is no discernible pattern. There is though, I tell myself. It's just not a straight pattern. But I look at where the other half of the labyrinth is supposed to be, a flat sheet of white snow, and realize how much of a fool's errand this seems. I know the labyrinth is deep beneath me, but it feels so inaccessible to me now. I nearly give up, thinking I will come back in a week or two when the snow is gone, but instead I trek on, "intently haphazard," unsure of where my next step is meant to go but determined to do my best to move toward the middle.

Isn't this what most of us are doing? Doing our best? Just putting the next foot forward? Isn't that how we get new families and institutions and churches and towns and communities? We look at the land beneath our feet and decide this looks good, we'll stay here, we'll keep doing this, even if it looks foolish to the world. Even the ones who leave our families and institutions and churches and towns and communities, isn't this what they're doing too? Just trying to do their best to do what seems best? Even if it takes an eternity?

7

HERE IS PROTECTION

NURSEMAIDS

So then, death is at work in us, but life is at work in you. . . . Therefore we do not lose heart. Though outwardly we are wasting away, yet inwardly we are being renewed day by day.

—2 Corinthians 4:12, 16

And for all this, nature is never spent;
There lives the dearest freshness deep down things.
—Gerard Manley Hopkins, "God's Grandeur"

One of the most challenging stretches of the Appalachian Trail is either on the first day of one's travels or on the last, depending on the direction one takes to complete the hike. Maine's tallest mountain, Katahdin, serves up a grueling hike destined to either defeat the day-one dreamer or deliver a satisfying end to a hike of a lifetime. In 1846, Henry David Thoreau visited an old-growth forest in the remote Katahdin and called it "grim and wild . . . savage and dreary."[1]

He was not alone in this estimation of the virgin American forest. When early American pilgrim William Bradford first saw an East Coast forest, he said it was "hideous and desolate . . . [with a] wild and savage hue."[2] French philosopher and scientist Alexis de Tocqueville called the American woods "forsaken" and "primaeval."[3] There is indeed a wildness in old growth that, in the right light, can seem almost otherworldly.

Lichen covers trees and branches; mosses drape over rocks and logs like lush carpets. William Wordsworth once said of such rocks that they were "fleeced with moss."[4] The moisture in the air and beneath one's feet brings a softness to the experience of walking in old growth. The canopy overhead lets streams of light through sparingly, and when its beams do come through, they seem to dance from the air particles moving through them. One rarely feels the need to shout in old growth; a whisper will almost always do.

Last autumn, when my friend Philip and I hiked back to the old-growth forest where Tree 103 fell, I was struck by how lush and green the forest floor was everywhere except where the canopy of Tree 103 was now missing. This ground— once green, gently watered by droplets falling through the pine boughs above, shaded by her broad branches, protected in winter by her snowy shingles—was already drying and brown. Ferns and moss and fungi and lichen flourish in the shade of old growth, but now there was sun pooling clear down where 103 once stood.

I know the trees around her will begin to slowly grow into her absence, rearranging themselves by degrees, pressing through and pushing out to find the sunlight and air, but that will take a long time, and I felt a little sad sitting there with my back against Tree 103. It was as though this stream of light is a tombstone of sorts for the tree that was, and tombstones are never preferred to the broken body below them.

Recently, I watched a short documentary on clear-cut logging practices in the Tongass National Forest in Alaska. A local girl who grew up under the old growth now weeps standing on a ten-foot-wide stump above acres of clear-cut forest. In the background, a politician opines about trees being "renewable resources" as he signs a bill to remove protections from the acres around the graveyard of trees. *What does it feel like*, I wish I could ask him, *to have lost your sense of wonder?*

Because I was watching the documentary on an aggregated video website, it recommended another documentary to me right away, this one a story about a small family who lives on Skid Row in California. They are also from Alaska, born and raised on welfare and methamphetamines, addiction ravaging their entire bloodline. Their sadness is palpable. No one dreams of being cut down when you've barely had time to exist. *This is what it looks like,* I think to myself, *to have your sense of wonder robbed from you.*

Many of these old-growth forests are four, five, six hundred years old, a thousand years old, even thousands. There is a Norwegian spruce in Fulufjället National Park in Sweden estimated to be over nine thousand years old, and it is, thank God, protected from chainsaws and mills. It is somewhat true that a tree is a renewable resource. Trees can be planted and grow again, only to be cut again. Forest managers and loggers do this all over the world, echoing farming practices: harvesting, then planting, moving to another forest, harvesting, then planting, and so on.

However, what old-growth forests provide in terms of carbon and carbon storage, oxygen, and nitrogen cannot be repeated in our lifetime. What they provide when they fall from natural old age and then sink into the earth below for centuries cannot be replicated. Similar to how fields that never experience crop rotation become depleted of necessary minerals and nutrients, causing erosion or more devastating effects, the clear-cut forest whose trees are hauled away to a sawmill is robbed of what is essential to make this resource *truly* renewable. It won't take three or four hundred years to heal these forests deep down beneath the roots; it will take a thousand.

Ecologist Robin Wall Kimmerer describes what happens after decimation like this to an old-growth forest:

> The early successional plant species arrive immediately and get to work on damage control. These plants—known as opportunistic, or pioneer, species—have adaptations that allow them to thrive after disturbance. Because resources like light and space are plentiful, they grow quickly. A patch of bare ground around here can disappear in a few weeks. Their goal is to grow and reproduce as fast as possible, so they don't bother themselves with making trunks, but rather madly invest in leaves, leaves, and more leaves borne on the flimsiest of stems.[5]

I am reminded of the foolish man who built his house on the sand, and when the winds and rain came, his house crumbled (see Matt. 7:24–27). The same will happen to these forests because flimsy stems and mere leaves do not have the intricate under- or above-ground systems to hold up whole landscapes. Without deep roots, without fungi, without the understory having something to grab hold of when the winds and rains come, it won't last long.

I once witnessed something called "breathing ground." Somehow the roots of a spindly tree had come ungrounded, but the tree had not yet fallen over. The spindly tree with the hair-thin roots, with all their dirt and moss and flimsy stems still attached, was being pulled up and set down as the wind blew the canopy above. Pulled back, set down, pulled back, set down. It had the appearance of a sleeping giant, his chest rising and falling rhythmically.

Though the ground had the appearance of breath, it was evidence of death.

Replanting clear-cut forests with a monoculture of new saplings doesn't provide the diversity and density that the forest needs in order to thrive. This may look like life, a renewable resource, but it's like planting tulips on someone's grave and insisting they're proof the human buried beneath them is still alive.

Last year Nate wrote in my birthday card, "I love your resiliency." I told him no one had ever called me resilient before. I desire it, but I do not feel it. I feel tender, easily bruised. I feel battered, easily dissuaded. I used to run away when I was pressed from any side. If something hurt, I flinched. If something pinched, I winced. I suppose this is the human condition, to withdraw from what pains us, but I wish I'd learned to work up some calluses a little earlier in life.

I was one of eight children, all boys except me, and I know every name there is for a girl who flinches from pain; I was called most of them by the time I was in middle school. One might think this would have made me resilient, but all it did was break me down. It made me tender to the world and humans and various views in ways that have tied me up in knots more than I'd like. It made me distrust my own hurt or pain, hopes or dreams. I always felt on the verge of being crushed. If there is any resiliency in me to be found, it is there only because I am so acutely aware of its absence and hold on to every shred when I can find it.

And so, during the crumbling and quaking of all the painful things in the past few years, I wanted to be resilient. I wanted to stand up strong and tough, certain and rooted. But deep within me, if I'm honest, what I mostly felt was just a cavernous tenderness, and some might call that weakness. I felt afraid. Afraid of people, afraid of judgments, afraid of disappointing others.

I wanted to defend my vote, my position on abortion and the death penalty and immigration and Black lives and climate change and gun reform and equal rights. I wanted to argue for what I thought was the most right (even if we couldn't know whether it was the ultimate best) position to take during the pandemic. I wanted to fight for the most vulnerable in my family, even while everyone they surrounded themselves with kept saying, "They're fine. Everything's fine. Look how fine they are. There's nothing to see here." But I don't believe in fine. I believe in getting to the root, and doing it sooner rather than later. I believe the answer to poverty and unwanted pregnancies and the prison population and school shootings and whole people groups wanting to come to America isn't just voting along a party line and hoping it goes your way. I believe that when we do something wrong, it is better to say, "I'm sorry," than to circle the wagons and cry, "Persecution!"

But mostly what I felt was weak and tender and small, barely there.

Nate and I are hiking up a mountain in the Adirondacks. It's not one of the forty-six High Peaks, but it has a clear view of many of them. There are a few trails to reach the summit, a rock face that is viewable from where we park our car along the road. We take the longer and less-steep trail to the top, just a few miles long. I am a slow hiker, owing to a combination of scarred lungs and the fact that "there's so much beauty for just two eyes to see."[6] I stop to spy on mushrooms and fiddlehead ferns, mosses and lichen. I pause for a bird call or to rest on a boulder. But mostly I'm looking for my favorite forest feature: nursemaids.

Some call them nurse logs or, if they're still rooted, nurse stumps. And although I'm sure it's akin to anthropomorphizing again, I've always called them nursemaids.

A nursemaid is a fallen tree from which new growth springs. In his Pulitzer Prize–winning novel, *The Overstory*, Richard Powers writes of these nurse logs, "A person has only to look, to see that dead logs are far more alive than living ones."[7]

"It looks like a fairy forest!" I say to Nate as I bend down to look at a log lying on the edge of the path. A two-inch balsam fir is just beginning to sprout from the carpet of spongy moss covering the nursemaid, in addition to orange jewelweed, a baby white pine, and another coniferous tree I don't know the name of yet. Fiddleheads are sprouting around the log, ready to provide a protective canopy for the perfect ecosystem below. Fungi cling to the sides of the log like nurses in neonatal intensive care units hovering around the babies, answering to their beck and call. The log is lush and spring green, wet to the touch, and beautiful in the eyes of this beholder.

Ecologists call the natural fall of a tree a "disturbance event" in the forest. Even though the fall may be quite natural—from old age, crowding, blight or rot from inside, weakening of the root system, or heavy winds—what happens when a tree falls can be quite disturbing to the forest.

Where Tree 103 used to stand, sunlight is now flooding a spot that hasn't seen this much light in hundreds of years. Any new growth that was in the path of the tree's fall was crushed beneath her. Roots around her were disturbed, wrenched from their secure beds.

Watch a houseplant lean toward the light in your living room. When one side begins to grow lopsided and heavy, turn the plant so the other side can photosynthesize and grow as tall as its neighbor. This happens in the forest too. Despite its name, a disturbance event is necessary for the good of the forest. It makes way for light to lean down to the forest floor where the log now lays. Scientists studying in Andrews Experimental Forest near Bend, Oregon (one the most primal forest ecosystems in the world), discovered that such "[nurse] logs are the most overlooked of the critical components of the living ecosystem."[8]

When campers and homeowners remove dry brush and logs to clear way for gardens or to use for campfires, it's a slight disturbance. But when the logging industry or forest service removes whole trees or whole landscapes, the land is robbed of its food for the next *several centuries*. One might even say the land is robbed of *ever* being renewed again because of the loss of a nurse log's singular ability to care for and cultivate new forest life *in its own death*. No one element of the forest can replicate the eons-long role of a nursemaid for the communal good of the forest.

Mary Oliver says of fallen trees and branches, "They lie on the ground and do nothing. They are travelers on the way to oblivion."[9] But is it really oblivion? One Andrews scientist says they "can prove that a fallen tree in an advanced stage of rot can hold far more mass of living tissue than a live and standing and apparently thriving one."[10] The singular purpose of that living tissue is to give life to the next generation of growth. Perhaps another name for these fallen trees could be legacy logs.

It is not the circumstances I find so difficult these days; rather, it's realizing that I've put my trust in people and institutions that have failed to be trustworthy. I thought I'd be able to sink my roots into the wisdom and integrity of those who came before me, but instead, when I look out at the landscape around me, it is clear-cut and bare, and the chances of renewal seem slim. And I have to ask myself: Do I want that monoculture to be renewed?

I never trusted the Republican Party, but I trusted the Christians around me who said character matters and so does life. But it seems to me now that they mostly meant fetal life and would attribute good character to anyone who echoed the message. I used to believe the church should be the safest place for the vulnerable, but now I see that many churches want vulnerable parishioners because they will be less likely to cause a ruckus when something goes wrong. I used to believe the older generation would know when it was their time to pass the baton to their children and grandchildren, to encourage them to pick up where they left off. But now their children and grandchildren are my peers and friends, and the older generations seem incapable of trusting us to do good work, perhaps because they believe our definition of good is too different from theirs. We care about poverty and the systems that catch people in their cycles, systems like mass incarceration and war-on-drugs policies that target racial minorities. We care about the earth, and we care about the children being gunned down in schools and stopping the madness that leads to it. We are called "woke" by our elders, and it isn't a kindness.

What makes me angry these days is that I thought we were protecting one another as a whole, but now I am learning we want to protect only the ones who look like us, vote like us, and choose like us. We want a monoculture, a homogenization of people.

A friend who left her church recently tells me through tears that another friend still in the church now calls her "extended family" instead of "family."

"You left," her friend says to her. "You chose to leave the family."

"I left because I love this church family too much to let this dysfunction and injustice continue to go unaddressed. It was my love that *led* me to leave."

"Too bad," her friend says. "By leaving you no longer are in a position to address any dysfunction."

I feel my skin crawl when I hear this language, this us-ing and them-ing, sounding more like a discussion between warring mafia families than between Christians, yet I am dividing people into us and them right this very second. I place my friend on a higher moral road than the road on which I place her friend. I *us* and *them* while I sit there listening to her. I almost cannot help it.

Last week I listened to an interview author Katherine May did with fellow author Emma Gannon. I pulled over the car to scribble down this insightful thing Gannon said about the othering we do: "We're social animals," she said, "and at the end of the day we go with the pack, we go with the herd of people who will harm us the least."[11]

This wasn't new information for me, but her way of saying it was: we go with the herd of people who will harm us the least.

At the end of it all, isn't this what we want? To not be harmed. To be safe. To be among those who echo us back to ourselves, who mirror us in likeness and being. Psychologist Curt Thompson says, "We are all born into the world looking for someone who's looking for us,"[12] and unless we consciously pull away from this desire for sameness, we will keep on gravitating to it throughout all of life.

It's not wrong to do this. I have always believed chemistry is found not just in sexual relationships but in friendships too. We survive as a species by working with one another, and how much better if we *like* working with one another too? But chemistry isn't the same as agreement. And agreement isn't the same as being looked for.

My oldest and dearest friend and I disagree deeply about many things—politics, theology, medical practices, and more. We talk almost every week, and it is rare when one or the other of us doesn't bring up some controversial subject. But our opinions don't divide us, because beneath it all—

the beliefs, the politics, the theology, the season of life—we are looking for one another. I will grope through the darkest night and deepest depths to find her because there is no one on earth except my husband who matters more to me. To understand her, to sometimes *work* to understand her, to see her as she truly is—and not just how she reflects me to myself—is some of my most meaningful work on earth.

This is what it means to protect one another, I think. It is laying aside our own glory or opinion or right and doing what it takes to let the other thrive within our presence. Apart from Nate, this friend is the safest person in my life, and I think she'd say a similar thing about me, not in spite of our disagreements but—in some ways—because we have learned that unity is more important than uniformity. And not some kumbaya unity either but a lichen kind of unity— different things in symbiosis for the betterment of the whole.

In the short story "Fidelity," Wendell Berry writes of the death of Burley Coulter, a beloved character in Port William, the idyllic community where most of Berry's fiction is based.

Burley is in a coma in the hospital after having lived his entire life in Port William, and his son Danny absconds with him to the woods where they once hunted and fished together. While Danny digs a grave for his father's impending death, mulling over their life together, a detective begins going door to door asking about the missing Burley, calling it a kidnapping. Every one of the locals feigns ignorance, and later that evening they convene at the lawyer's office, where the lawyer Wheeler is illuminating the detective on Burley Coulter's life. Wheeler says, "A man has disappeared out of your world, Mr. Bode, that he was never in for very long. And you don't know where, and you don't know how. He has disappeared into his people and his place, not to be found in this world again forever."[13]

Berry is fictionalizing what he wrote in his essay "Health Is Membership," in which he posits that only in belonging *to* something or someone can we be healthy. The thing he thinks we ought to belong to is a community like Port William—small, local, and generational. He says, "Like divine love, earthly love seeks plenitude; it longs for the full membership to be present and to be joined."[14]

This "full membership" has always made me curious, made me wonder. What does it mean to belong to something or someone fully? How can we do it in such a way that it is not hierarchal but communal? Is trying to unite different things to each other doomed to failure? Will we always become less of ourselves when united or just more of one another? Is it possible to be a part of a community without agreeing with the community on the most salient things? Is it good for us to become so entangled with one another that it's hard to tell where one of us stops and another begins?

Next time you go for a hike, pay attention to the people you pass coming back down the mountain. Almost without exception they will say to you, "You're almost there!" or "It's worth it!" or you will say to them, "Is it worth it?" or "Almost there?" It is the universal conversation of hikers. We can't help connecting with one another over both the journey and the destination. The great conservationist Aldo Leopold says of the forest, "All ethics rest upon a single premise: that the individual is a member of a community of interdependent parts."[15] Sometimes all I need to continue on is the "you've got this" fist bump from someone who got there first.

Nate and I are nearing the top of the peak. I can tell because the air is growing colder and the alpine plants and mosses are more plenteous. I love the look of club moss, which is not really a moss at all but part of the fern family. It lies like a forest of tiny pine trees across the forest floor and pokes through ground rock.

The path grows less and less defined here because the ground is becoming more solid granite than soil. Cairns— short stacks of stones and rocks placed by park rangers to stop hikers from veering off the path—are our only source of direction. We scramble up a final rock face surrounded by short, stumpy trees that can weather some of the highest-recorded winds in the Northeast, and we emerge onto a wide, granite summit. We are surrounded by green mountains on every side, the wind whipping us backward. In the middle of the summit is another cairn, this one more of a monument than a compass, as if those who summited the peak wished to leave their mark. I stand next to it and place my own pebble atop it. The cairn rivals me for size and can't handle much more.

We duck down into a little cove in the rock face where the trees give a little more protection but the view is still spectacular, and we sit there for a while, breathing in the scent of balsam.

We came out here today because the grief was pounding us hard, the disorientation of the past season had caught up with us. We needed to be outside in something bigger and more substantial than us. I cried in the car on the way here, tears of anger and sorrow and fear and confusion. I want to abandon America. I want to leave the church. I want nothing to do with politics. I am weary of the pandemic. I am heartbroken for what my family is going through. I am tired of myself and being by myself and yet feel like I can't trust anyone except myself. I am learning to trust the still, small voice of my gut and my God, but none of it feels sufficient in the face of so much loss. I want the protection of a community I can count on and leaders I can look to and values that are immovable. But when I look around and within and above, all I can see is the companionship of Jesus. Apart from two things, a secure home and a safe marriage, I am finding my orientation around one thing only: Jesus.

A friend said to me recently, "I thought all this time my faith was in Jesus, but it turns out it was mostly in institutions and people, and now that so many of them are crumbling, I am having to face this about myself." I haven't stopped thinking about this since he said it to me. Me too, friend. Me too. And in facing this loss of certainty in institutions and people, I'm having to face myself, including my own complicity in propping up those spaces. Who am I, I ask, when I am completely untethered from a political party or a church denomination or a group of friends or a popular position on a fraught issue? Perhaps I should have been able to answer this years ago, but I don't think I've ever felt so alone before and so I don't think I've been so forced to think about it.

Here, in this rock cove, next to the man I love, sheltered by the stubby trees to our sides and the rock to our back, I feel protected from the winds. I feel solid and sure. And I feel still. I am still. I am here and I am still and I am less afraid of what I will find out about myself than I used to be.

Spiritual writer Parker Palmer writes in his book *A Hidden Wholeness*, "I have been astonished to see how nature uses devastation to stimulate new growth, slowly but persistently healing her own wounds."[16] Robin Wall Kimmerer says it's not always so easy though. Writing about our dear Adirondack forests, she says, "It turns out that when forests around here grow back after agricultural clearing, the trees come back readily, but the understory plants do not."[17] Some trees and plants do use devastation to renew themselves—this is why controlled burns in forests can greatly encourage new growth. But not everything will come back.

Not all wounds will be healed. Not all scars will disappear. Not everything is renewable or replicable.

In the absence of old-growth logs in which to sink my fragile roots, I find myself looking for new friendships and environments. We are looking for a new church since we moved. We are getting to know our new neighbors. We are inviting new perspectives. All my life I've sought out the places and people who felt the most like me, but now I find myself looking for something and someone different.

I no longer want to live in a house of mirrors, where every human reflection—though distorted—still resembles me. I want a museum, a portrait gallery, a library, where every bit of my world is distinct and beautiful in its own right. I am learning not to look for ways to be on the same page but instead to envision the wholly distinct story of another's life and work.

Instead of asking, "How closely do we align?" I am learning to ask, "How much room is there in this relationship or environment for those who disagree?" I am learning to ask, "Can we disagree and still—somehow—grow together as neighbors?"

This is a new way for me to be; it feels uncomfortable sometimes. My listening skills will have to activate. I will need to ask more questions. I will need to refrain from labeling others with labels they wouldn't give themselves. I will need to refrain from labeling myself at times too. I have seen the effects of a monoculture, and I know the patience it takes for diversity to grow and thrive, how it means letting what has fallen remain so, how it means that I may have to fall myself too.

In some old-growth forests, one may see spindly, spider-like legs supporting a whole tree above them. They are called "buttresses," and Daniel Matthews writes about them in his book on the Cascades. He says:

> By age ten or sooner, a seedling extends fine rootlets down the nurse log's sides to mineral soil, even from perches 20′ up on snag tops. Over the decades, if the seedling survives, the rootlets grow into sturdy "prop roots" while the nurse log slowly rots out from underneath. You can see this process at all stages; at some point the support relationship may reverse, a few chunks of rotting nurse now dangling from the prop roots. Over the course of two to six centuries, the nurse log disappears and the tree's roots fill in, remaining as "buttresses" on the lower trunk of a huge spruce, hemlock, or Douglas-fir.[18]

The once tall tree, now fallen and decomposed, is still saying *adsum*.

I was here.

I am here.

My contribution to the forest is still visible even if I am long gone.

There is a word used in song when the Lord brings his people through yet another trial. The word is *dayenu*, meaning something along the lines of "and if nothing else, it would have been enough." If the Lord had merely fed us during the famine but not given us a home in Egypt, it would have been enough. If the Lord had given us a home in Egypt but not kept us from being enslaved, it would have been enough. If the Lord had brought us out of Egypt but not parted the Red Sea, it would have been enough. If the Lord had parted the Red Sea but not brought every last one of us through it, it would have been enough. This was their way of saying, "No matter what the future is, what you've done for us is enough."

In the book of Samuel, when the Israelites defeat the Philistines, Samuel takes a stone and sets it up, calling it Ebenezer, saying, "Thus far the LORD has helped us" (1 Sam. 7:12). It is a physical representation of *dayenu*.

I scoop up a small pile of stones and build a miniature cairn in that cove on top of the mountain. "Thus far," I say to myself. This far. I wish I'd come to these realizations sooner, but I didn't. And now I have. Therefore, this far have I come. I am here. Here I am.

I pick up a few more stones and pocket them, willfully disregarding the leave-no-trace principle. The truth is I have been here. I am here. *Adsum.* I will be here again. I cannot help but leave a trace of where I have been. The disturbance event has happened, whether I like it or not. The chasm has happened. The breaking has happened. The realization is here. I cannot unsee what I see about our country and our world and the church and our communities and my family and my own self.

At home, I build another small cairn on a shelf above my desk, a reminder that I'm here thus far but also that my work now is to leave a trail for others behind me, replete with markers for the way forward. My work is to become a fallen tree upon which new forests grow.

PART 3

REVEALED

8

HERE IS EMERGENCE
WEEDS

**For our light and momentary troubles are achieving for us
an eternal glory that far outweighs them all.**

—2 Corinthians 4:17

> I want you to stand among strangers, all young
>   and ephemeral to you,
> Silently keeping the secret of your birth.
>
>   —Dana Gioia, "Planting a Sequoia"

The beavers are at war with me. Or perhaps it is I who is
at war with them. Over the spring they have leveled the
shoreline between the giant river willows standing sentry at
the corners of our property line. They've taken the blackthorn and poplar shoots and the new willow saplings too,

none of which we planted but all of which we hoped to watch grow. But in an incendiary act of violence, one early spring night a few weeks ago, they padded up across the riverbank and onto our lawn, slicing neatly through the river birch trees we planted three autumns before. The birch bark was just turning white and peeling, the trees having sunk their roots beside the river that kept them fed and watered. They had doubled in size over the past few years, and we had no idea that while we watched in delight as their canopy spread, another species was also watching, waiting for their trunks to reach optimum width for their own purposes.

There is a graveyard of spindly stumps along our shoreline now; the giant beaver dam in an inlet across from our house has been solidly fortified.

There are plenty of other shorelines, acres and acres of them along the river, plenty of public land that isn't inhabited by humans. Why did they choose to demolish ours?

This isn't my first run-in with beavers. A few years ago, I was out on my kayak at night, stargazing in the pitch black, and from less than a kayak's length away a shocking slap sounded and sent a series of waves toward me, destabilizing my kayak. I tried to paddle away, but "away" was a misnomer because I couldn't see where the beaver was and was about to realize that there was more than one circling me. I moved toward home, followed by the indignant slaps echoing across the water reminding me it was I who was in their territory, and not they in mine.

But I respected them, didn't I? I left and have steered clear of their giant dam ever since. Couldn't they afford me the same kindness? Apparently not.

And so now our river view is less obstructed, which sounds nice in theory, but I am of the mindset that the less we interfere with what grows, the better. If I had my druthers, we'd stop mowing the side yard completely and let the grasses and native plants take over outside our fenced yard. Joan Maloof, ecologist and author of *Teaching the Trees*, writes, "Forest is our land's natural calling."[1] If that's true, then I suppose the beavers might argue they are our land's natural landscapers.

The idea of proper landscaping has always made me feel a little twitchy. For years I lived in the suburban sprawl of the Dallas–Fort Worth metroplex, where nearly every lawn looked the same or at least shared similar elements. Once I pushed the limits of our local HOA by planting a small, kidney-shaped wildflower garden in our front yard—unheard of in our neighborhood. The thing about wildflowers is they often look a little (or a lot) like weeds until they look like flowers. The first year a few neighbors complained anonymously, so I edged the kidney with brick pavers, hoping the boundary lines would put them at ease. I wondered aloud to the sheepish HOA officer who came with our third citation, "Who gets to decide what is and what isn't an acceptable plant?"

Michael Pollan, in his book *Second Nature*, writes about the hierarchy of weeds and plants, saying, "At the top stand the hypercivilized hybrids—think of the rose, 'queen of the garden'—and at the bottom are the weeds, the plant world's proletariat, furiously reproducing and threatening to usurp the position of their more refined horticultural betters. Where any given plant falls in this green chain of being has a lot to do with fashion, but there are a few abiding rules. In general, the more intensively a plant has been hybridized—the further it's been distanced from its wildflower origins—the higher its station in plant society."[2]

No one in the suburbs ever complained about my rambling rose bushes or their neighboring neatly squared-off hedges, just the wildflowers.

What is it about wildness that makes us uncomfortable?

After being away from home for ten days in the beginning of May, Nate and I came home to mid-calf-height grass and a prolific amount of weeds in the garden. Proletariats indeed. My first free day I donned my boots and baseball cap, sprayed some expensive bug spray that swears to ward off all the bugs with none of the chemicals, and marched out to the garden armed with a weed bucket and spade. I spent the entire day out there, coming inside only to refill my water glass. Our garden is not large in the grand scheme of things, but I moved slowly, resolutely, patiently.

Ralph Waldo Emerson once said something like a weed is a thing whose virtues haven't yet been discovered.[3] My mother-in-law, a master gardener, says a weed is a plant that's just in the wrong place—the inference being that only you determine its rightful place. I picked through the perennials that were just creeping up through last year's shorn stems and pulled the aggressive, creeping weeds that decidedly *were* in the wrong place. I left the wild phlox and the clover, all interspersed with irises and columbine and the waning dark maroon, nearly black tulips. I pulled away the limp and dried stalks of ornamental tall grasses and rediscovered a little community of astilbe I'd forgotten about.

Wendell Berry, in a documentary about his life, says of what we might call weeds, "The world is also full of people who would rather pay for something to kill the dandelions than to appreciate the dandelions. Well, I'm a dandelion man myself."[4]

I've scrawled the words "I'm a dandelion man" on index cards and in margins more times than I can count, a way of reminding myself that what may seem like a weed (or wild, or inconvenient, or just uncomfortable) is a matter of perspective. We've heard it said that beauty is in the eye of the beholder, and we might find more beauty in the world if we stopped trying to decide what everyone else must find beautiful and just enjoyed what we ourselves do.

While I want to be a dandelion man in principle, I pulled out every last dandelion in my garden by its long, thin root, cupping their seedy heads in my hands as I put them in the weed bucket so their kind didn't proliferate further.

Last week I noticed a tiny maple sapling emerging in the shade garden next to our house, and I wonder what will happen if I just leave it there. Will I regret it? Will it become a towering maple in a hundred years, its roots upending the porch addition we just put in place? For now I leave it because *behold, it is*. Who am I to tell it otherwise?

We were away for ten days because I just finished a master's in theology degree from a university a thousand miles away. I don't know what exactly that means for me, and I know less than I did when I began the graduate program. I spent almost a decade trying to land on a graduate program that resonated with me, but I was finding that most theological institutions tended toward a particular denomination or drew a certain kind of theological type to their programs. I knew that if I went to a Baptist seminary or a Presbyterian one, a Lutheran or Episcopal one, I would very likely leave holding an advanced degree and very little love for God or the church.

I know this about myself: I cannot flourish in a monoculture. I need diversity of ideas and persons because it keeps me from sinking into a stupor of belief that the loudest voices in my ears must be the right ones. I am too easily lulled to slumber without the friction of competing ideas and methods. When I finally chose a program, I chose an ecumenical one, one where both the faculty and the students would be coming from diverse perspectives and theological environments.

I knew this would keep me from going through the motions, but what I didn't anticipate was that this would strip away many of the preconceived notions I came in with. Coming in, I resonated in theory with what we in the program called "generous orthodoxy," but in practice I still felt certain things were more right than others. I also didn't anticipate leaving the program with a more solid and singular foundation on Jesus and a more open hand toward all the things that orient around Jesus, including theology.

Who gets to choose what stays and what goes? And what if what goes in another's space stays in one's own? Or vice versa? If enough of us claim to believe in absolute truth, then some of us are going to have to be getting it wrong because we can't all be right. This is a point philosophers and theologians have wrestled with for eons, and I can't even attempt to address its complexities here.

Pilate asked Jesus, who stood before him in torn robes, "What is truth?" (John 18:38). And while some might dismiss the question as the philosophical meanderings of a lazy mind that prefers to debate instead of land, I tend to think it was rather the question of a person who wanted to know and yet, down deep within, wrestled with settling on just one truth. I know that person because I am that person. This is one of the things I know, without doubt, to be true.

It is a rainy Wednesday morning, Nate is upstairs nursing a cold, and my tea is half drunk when my phone lights up with a text from a friend: "The rain is magical . . . want to go hiking?" I don't hesitate and type back, "I'm in. What time?" We agree on a time (as soon as we both get our rain gear on) and a destination (a nearby old-growth forest that edges a pond and bog), and twenty minutes later he picks me up and we're on our way.

We drive past the entrance to a local state park, make a few turns as the trees grow larger and the forest grows darker, then head down a few logging roads and up a short hill, past a bend in the road that hikers have filled with cairns of varying sizes and shapes, hundreds of them. A bit later he pulls over the car. We pull on our raincoats and step out of the car and into a bed of knee-high maidenhead ferns. It is pouring now, but we don't mind a bit. The bugs won't be biting, and it will be cooler.

The hike up is a steep grade littered with ferns and trillium and tiny saplings of all sorts. Giant boulders with chips of crystal on their shoulders permeate the ridge line. They are covered with mosses, and ferns drip down their sides like waterfalls. We boulder hop for a while, running our hands over the beds of moss and bits of lichen clinging to their sides. A few times one of us steps on a nursemaid, and it's so decomposed that our foot crushes it down. We're picking our steps carefully. There is no trail, and I wonder with every footfall who has stepped here, right here, before. When did they step here? And why?

I call ahead to my friend with the words of a Robert Shaw poem about moss, "Not so much groundcover as ground-hugger,"[5] and I wish I could hug the moss, sleep on it. My friend is days away from taking a weekend course on moss at the local forestry college. I'm envious and tell him I'll live vicariously through him.

Why am I not taking the course with him? Because today, as I am running my hands over moss and gasping over old growth, I was supposed to be on the other side of the country, on a trip through a series of national parks. Nate and I had planned the trip for months, meticulously routing our path, scheduling campsites, sorting out a menu, reserving stretches of roads or hikes or walks accessible only to those who planned in advance. The night before we were supposed to leave for our seven-week-trip, we received some medical news that ended the trip before it began. We unpacked our car and trailer, unloaded our tent and camping stove, emptied the coolers and water jugs. Just as meticulously as I'd planned and reserved everything, I went through and canceled it all. Planning the trip took months; unplanning it took less than twenty-four hours.

So instead I will live vicariously through my friend as he learns about moss varieties and rubs shoulders with those who've dedicated their lives to the study of what one poet calls "the slipcover of rocks"[6] and another calls "an old-fashioned doormat."[7]

We bushwhack our way down to the small pond, talking about a time he kayaked on it and saw loons. Loons are another love we share. "Loons?" I exclaim. "But it's not deep enough." They prefer deeper water, diving into depths nearing 250 feet in search of food. "This pond can't be more than fifteen or twenty feet," I say.

"I know," he replies. "That's what made it so surprising and special."

After that I keep one ear pondside, hoping to hear the mournful call of a loon in search of his mate.

We emerge from the thick growth on a small hill sitting above the pond. The view wouldn't be much to most people, a small body of water edged with bogs and bushes and beaver dams. It's too foggy to see what's in the distance, and overall it's a fairly unimpressive view. But my friend and I are easily impressed because there, in front of us, is a giant wild huckleberry bush that has to be nearly a hundred years old, and next to it is a wild blueberry bush rivaling it for size. To the north, we can see an ancient larch that looks dead up top but is impressively feeding a whole ecosystem with its roots. Everywhere we look there are ferns unfurling from their fiddleheads. Dainty maidenheads shoot up from the floor and curtsy to their neighbors. Ramps and bloodroot press up through the carpet of last year's dropped leaves. Burgeoning firs and maples, beeches and birches defer to one another for the limited sunlight in this boreal forest. Hobblebush and hardhack and bog laurel and dogbane proliferate the floor around us.

We sit on the wet, cushiony hilltop and just watch for a while. I am sure, as sure as I can be, that we are the only ones who have ever sat here before and seen these native plants take the earth captive on a rainy Wednesday morning in May.

I welcome the wildness.

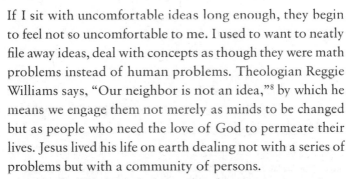

If I sit with uncomfortable ideas long enough, they begin to feel not so uncomfortable to me. I used to want to neatly file away ideas, deal with concepts as though they were math problems instead of human problems. Theologian Reggie Williams says, "Our neighbor is not an idea,"[8] by which he means we engage them not merely as minds to be changed but as people who need the love of God to permeate their lives. Jesus lived his life on earth dealing not with a series of problems but with a community of persons.

Instead of labeling whole swaths of groups in or out, Jesus met the lame man at the temple and the woman at the well and the father of the demoniac and the bleeding woman and the cheating tax collector and the begging children and the self-righteous leaders and the zealots and centurions and lepers. He didn't categorize a person based on what they did for work or did to survive or did because it's all they ever knew to do. He encountered them just as they were, there in front of him, and helped them to belong more wholly or to move to a space where they could flourish. His whole ministry was one of saying, "You have been there, but I came to put you here. Here—in me—is where you will thrive and bloom and belong."

So I am asking myself these days, how do I encounter people's ideals and principles, the sort that used to gird up my communities and values and votes and decisions and, instead of seeing them as incontrovertible facts, separate the opinion from the person? Can I see who these people are apart from what they have done or left undone?

This morning I read a review of a recently released book written by a worker in women's healthcare. According to the review, the book's author celebrates the choice that pregnant mothers make to abort. There were lines in the review that once would have made me want to throw it across the room or come up with some scathing or sarcastic response. But instead, I read the piece in its entirety, I held my judgments at bay, I tried to hear the reviewer's positive perspective of the book and the author's perspective. I could see the language they both used and how conditioned it had been by their lived experiences and the communities of which they'd been a part. I could also see that they genuinely believed they were right and that their belief in a woman's right to choose what she does with her body (put aside, for a moment, the fact that their choice also affects the body of another) was motivated by virtue and goodness.

She is not a monster, and they are not murderers. They care deeply about women. They care about their own children. They care about vulnerable demographics like victims of rape and incest. It wasn't difficult at all to see the degree of care that went into their words about a choice many Americans nonetheless intensely despise.

It is incredibly difficult, however, for me to see that same humanity and care in someone who made a decision that hurt my own vulnerable family members. The clergy who were tasked to care for my family neglected to report their abuse and kept it quiet for four years before someone else found out and reported it. It has taken all my willpower over the past two years to continue seeing them as people who care about the vulnerable and whose motivations are rooted in a form of virtue and goodness. The fact that I want to add a caveat every sentence of this paragraph shows that I am not yet at the point I want to be where I can believe that as wholeheartedly as I believe it about the writers mentioned above. But I am working to believe it.

I disagree deeply with these two ideals, the choice to abort a child and the choice to handle child abuse accusations in-house instead of reporting them to authorities. Those who hold to either one of these values may not see their value on par with the other, but I do. To me they are of equal importance and value to the heart of God.

Do you see how complex this is? It isn't easy. It isn't neat. But instead of pretending this complexity doesn't exist or acting like it's an uninvited guest, I make room for it instead. Asking the question "What is true?" does not mean I am, like Pilate, condemning Jesus to his death. I know that only a few verses before Pilate asks that question, Jesus weathers a similar struggle in the garden alone with his Father, asking in essence, "Can you be trusted? Is this really true? Is it really happening?" I find I don't trust the people who say all things are simple, easy, that there is one way of being or believing, one way of voting or promoting. I don't trust those who make it seem easy. I want to welcome the wildness, the complexity.

"Bushwhack, verb: to travel by foot through uncleared terrain; to clear a path or advance through thick woods especially by chopping down bushes and low branches."[9] Some people call it free hiking; others call it all in a day's work. My friend and I decide to bushwhack around the bog to a small, cascading waterfall on the north side of the pond and then follow the brook down to the road where the car is parked. It will not be an easy hike, but we are already soaked through in every layer and the day isn't half over, and there will be so much more to see.

The brush is thick and wet. There is no telling where our feet will land next or if they'll land on solid ground. Every wet log is a death trap, and every mossy rock is a gamble. It is always a tough decision for me when in the forest: Do I look down or up? There is so much to see in both spaces. But here the choice is clear: keep my eyes on wherever my foot will fall next.

No one decides what is a weed in an uncultivated forest. Each plant is where it is meant to be. Everything that can grow there will grow there, their seeds carried by wind or birds or the feet of various mammals who make their way through. Look around the bottom of an old tree and notice how beneath its canopy it feeds its young, nurturing them and shading them until maybe one of the saplings makes it to maturity. Notice the shape of every green thing you see, the leaves, the stems, the spindly shoots, the moss and lichen and fungi. Notice how it is all distinct and different and no one is telling it where to go or where not to go. It grows where it wills, and there it will grow until something other competes better for its space or sunshine or nutrients. John Luoma writes, "Communities of species move through a sort of community evolution, at each successional stage laying a biological foundation for the next, and simultaneously for their own demise."[10]

That last line, "simultaneously for their own demise," caught me when I first read it months ago. Plant life may be one of the only things in the world that does not uproot and leave in order to be "among those who will harm them the least." Instead, it stands resolute until it either takes over or something else takes over it—either way, it did what it was meant to do, even if someone else might have called it a weed or a nuisance or wild.

In Henry David Thoreau's seminal essay "Walking," there is the oft-quoted line, "Wildness is the preservation of the world." But Thoreau goes on, "Every tree sends its fibers forth in search of the wild."[11] As much as we have been made to cultivate, something in us reaches forth in search of the wild. But that desire has a competing one. It is at war with a need for order, to make sense, to compartmentalize and cultivate and categorize, and this is why it's so easy to think of our neighbor as an idea instead of as a human.

A human is made of flesh and blood, unpredictable tempers and personalities, heartbreaking stories and wild hopes and dreams. They are a part of an ecosystem they didn't create and are also creating an ecosystem simply by virtue of living and breathing. They exist, they are here, they are not unimportant, they matter. But their mattering clashes violently at times with our mattering and the things that matter to us. It is difficult to share space with something so foreign to us.

A friend and I just spent a few hours catching up. We usually talk every week, but it had been a few weeks because we kept missing each other. We stumbled into a topic on which we land in different places. In most friendships, with this topic, the habit is to fight or flee when it comes up. It's a tough one in our political and religious climate. But we endeavor, as we always do, to practice curiosity with each other. We ask, "How did you come to this view? What is it about this view that resonates with your story or personality? Are you willing to be wrong?" Or we ask ourselves, "Am I willing to be wrong? Why? Or why not? What is the incontrovertible truth upon which I am basing my opinion?"

In this friendship, we are enlarging the tent of our relationship and our capacity for differences by engaging with the other not merely as an idea or a monoculture, a product of a church or environment, but as a human we love and want to understand, and whom we want to be understood by. This is not easy work. This is cultivating work. Our aim is not to create another monoculture but to embrace the diversity that will preserve our world and preserve our faith in the one in whom we can absolutely agree.

As my hiking friend and I begin the wet descent down the side of the waterfall, I feel a tickle in my throat and an overwhelming tiredness.

Maybe I'm dehydrated, I think.

"Maybe I'm dehydrated," I say.

But a few hundred feet from the car, I realize it's more than dehydration. Within hours, I've spiked a fever and lost my sense of taste and smell.

Nate and I take tests the next morning, and we are both positive for COVID-19. We hunker down to recover with fluids and a series of documentaries. Less than a week later, though, a pain in my stomach and several hours of violent vomiting signal something else is wrong. In the emergency room, we learn I have appendicitis and will be taken in for surgery that morning.

"When it rains it pours," I tell a friend.

A few days later, still positive for COVID and recovering from surgery, I see my hiking friend pull up in our driveway holding a potted plant in his arms. I'm sitting on our porch and can see it's a pot full of maidenhead ferns, the very ones we talked about digging up and transplanting when we were hiking the week before, the ones we waded through on our rainy day bushwhack.

He plonks the pot down in a shady, wet spot of our north-facing garden, and I ask, "You think it will grow here?"

"I don't know," he says. "Can't hurt to try."

What would it hurt to try to rebuild a diverse ecosystem in the church and world? What harm could it do to just *try* to be with those who see the world differently than we do? Could it hurt? Maybe. Might some of us be crushed? Possibly. Will all of us survive? Unlikely.

Could we choose to build diverse and robust communities full of people with diverse and robust convictions and ideas and stories? Could we decide in advance that we will not demonize the different or cauterize the conflicts? Could we embrace the dandelions and clovers and even the thistles for what they bring—even if the only thing they bring is something unexpected, something a little different, something a little wild?

9

HERE IS RESILIENCE

MYCELIA

So we fix our eyes not on what is seen, but on what is unseen, since what is seen is temporary, but what is unseen is eternal.

—2 Corinthians 4:18

The trees encountered on a country stroll
Reveal a lot about a country's soul.

—W. H. Auden, "Woods"

We woke to the smell of woodsmoke and a thick veil of orange having fallen over our community. By midmorning the sun was a pinprick of bright pink in an otherwise gray sky.

By noon the light casting shadows in our house was a warm gold, as though someone had put a sepia filter on our world.

As the crow flies, we live about fifteen miles from the Canadian border, and just over the border, fires have been raging.

The smoke curved slowly downward in a widening spiral, reaching across the Saint Lawrence Seaway and then Lake Ontario and then over to us and the Adirondack Park. That evening it made its way downstate, into New York City and Philadelphia, widening its spiral. By morning Washington, DC, was wrapped in a cloak of orange, and by noon it had reached down into Virginia and North Carolina. News outlets warned us to stay inside with our windows closed and air purifiers on, to don N95 masks if we went outside. The *New York Times* said one day of breathing this air was akin to smoking one pack of cigarettes.

Nate and I were still recovering from COVID, so staying home and limiting ourselves to our upstairs, where the air purifiers kept the air clearer, felt fairly easy. But less than a hundred miles north, the fires were out of control and all hands were on deck fighting them.

Forest fires have become almost commonplace in some parts of the country—namely, the Pacific Northwest. Occasionally, even the smoke from those fires will make it to the East Coast, but we rarely have our own fires to contend with. The eerie pall cast over the whole Northeast this week proliferated everyone's social media, including my own. It's an abnormality for us.

It is only a few weeks into summer and we're already in a drought, also abnormal for this part of the country, known for humid summers and snowy winters. The tightly regulated water levels of the river that runs past our house signal to all who live along it that there's probably a burn ban too. When the river's high, we're good. When it's low, any spark could light these woods on fire.

There hasn't been an unchecked wildfire in the Adirondacks for more than a hundred years. In the early 1900s, two burned nearly six hundred thousand acres, and since then all fires have been tightly controlled. It helps that the forests of the Adirondacks are so diverse. In a place where trees are less protected by diverse neighbors, fires burn hotter and faster. Forester and ecologist Suzanne Simard writes, "In most years in Canada, more carbon is lost to wildfire than from the burning of fossil fuels, and we should be trying to reduce the risk by planning for landscapes of mixed forest instead of coniferous forest and for corridors of birch and aspen to serve as firebreaks because their leaves are moister and less resinous than those of conifers."[1] Though the majority of the trees in these mountains are conifers, the Adirondacks are also rife with birch, aspen, alder, and beech, as well as a thick undergrowth of shrubs and plants. Despite the lack of rain, the prolific vegetation acts as a bit of a protective shield— for now—for these woods, coniferous and deciduous alike.

The beavers aren't the only ones who want to take down the birch. For decades, foresters like Simard and her logging family had thought of birch and aspen and alder trees like weeds, threats to the pine and fir plantations they planted after clear-cutting for wood. It wasn't until Simard began studying the data—over nearly forty years—that she realized these trees are actually friends of the tall pines and Douglas firs that the logging industry so desperately desires, that they help coniferous trees grow straighter, taller, stronger, and with fewer knots.

After running various experiments over decades, Simard became the first ecologist to discover a vast underground network of mycorrhizal fungi. This network provides a pipeline between trees of various species sharing both carbon and nitrogen in a symbiotic relationship. She called it "mutualism,"[2] imagining the relationship between birch and fir as "weaving a network as brilliant as a Persian rug."[3] Years earlier, Jon Luoma had written in his book *The Hidden Forest*, "Fungi provide an absolutely vital—even life saving—role for the trees,"[4] but the nature of their role remained a mystery until Simard's breakthrough experiments.

Simard's work has inspired documentaries like *Fantastic Fungi*, Peter Wohlleben's bestselling book *The Hidden Life of Trees*, and my favorite character in Richard Powers's *The Overstory*.

As I write this, our former president is being indicted with thirty-seven charges against him. His approval ratings have already been high among his base, but I say to Nate that I fear his legal troubles will only embolden his supporters further in the culture war they've declared.

Nate and I were two of millions who, in 2015 and 2016, thought a Trump presidency would never happen. I will never forget watching the votes come in the night of the 2016 election and the slow, creeping dread that worked its way over me. I couldn't believe what I was witnessing. I hadn't called myself a Republican for years, but almost everyone I knew and loved voted that way—some more vocally than others. It was the first time I thought to myself, *I actually have no idea what the Republican Party is anymore. I don't know these people like I thought I did.*

For months after the election, I felt shell-shocked by the people I knew and had trusted who rejoiced at Trump's impending presidency. I muted and hid person after person after person on my social media feeds. I knew most of these people to be not only antiabortion but also faithful, kind, churchgoing, Bible-reading humans who seemed to me to be more well-rounded than a "one-issue voter" would be. I was earnestly trying to fit the picture I had of them into the picture I had of the president-elect, and I struggled to do it. The disorientation made, and still makes, my head hurt.

Four years later, then, I felt I understood the disorientation many of those same people felt when they learned my vote would be going to the candidate most likely to defeat Trump. And their even further disorientation over the fact that I not only was going to vote for him but also actually agreed with more of his policies—though not all of them—than the policies of the Republican Party. Now I was the one being muted, hidden, ignored, unfriended, and dismissed.

Rumors circulated that I didn't take sin seriously. Old friends texted saying that I promoted the "murdering of babies," that I was an "enemy of life." I knew they were wrong—my pro-all-life ethic is stronger than ever—but I also felt a deep empathy for their inability to envision my vote for the party they loathed. Over the past four years, our world had become even more disintegrated—dis-integrated. We were more divided than ever, and anyone who was on the "other side" of anything wasn't just wrong; they were to be demonized and criticized and marginalized. The isolationism and political pandering that happened during the pandemic only made everyone who was "other" seem bigger and badder than before.

It is easier to pretend there are monsters in our closets and under our beds if we refuse to look at what's really there—or not there, as the case usually is.

I do not look forward to the coming election year, but I wonder, *What can I do this time around to make it different for my community and me?*

I have always had a healthy relationship with fire. I grew up around campfires, and my father was a volunteer fire-fighter. We were well versed in what to do when fire became a problem. But there's a difference between controlled fire and uncontrolled fire.

Last autumn, as Nate and I were getting ready for bed, we let Harper out for her last foray around the yard. Within minutes she was sprayed by a skunk, but we didn't know it until she was back inside. We sprang into action mode, gathering supplies to bathe her and de-skunk our house.

Nate put her in the garage and ran to our next-door neighbors for their de-skunking shampoo. I ran into the kitchen and reached under the cabinet for some white vinegar to simmer on our stove to neutralize the scent. We met back in the mudroom to decide what to do next. Within seconds, though, the simmering pot on the stove was in flames, four feet tall, licking the low ceilings of our 1800s house. We both froze. Logic would have said to cover the pot, but instead I grabbed a bag of flour (I later learned this is not what to do) and dumped it over the fire. That only made the situation worse. It never occurred to us to find the pot's lid, and I'm still not sure why we thought it was a good idea to lift the pot and take it outside. Reader, never do this. *Never do this*.

As soon as I opened the door, a gust of wind blew the fire—still billowing out of the pot—back toward Nate's arm and face. He threw the pot, with all its fiery liquid, away from him, where the liquid landed in twenty spots all over our front porch, including on my feet and legs. "My feet are on fire!" I screamed. Meanwhile, Nate was on his hands and knees lifting up rugs and trying to smother the spots of fire. I knelt on a bench to extinguish the fire on my feet and then ran to help him put out all the little fires.

This all happened within less than a minute. Probably less than forty seconds. Uncontrolled fire. We were flummoxed about how it happened. Fire is not usually a response to vinegar. Was the skunk smell somehow flammable? Enough to light a fire of that magnitude? We didn't take the time to think about it. We texted some other neighbors that we were heading to the emergency room to get our burns treated, and they messaged back that they would be over to bathe Harper until she was clean. I will never underestimate the value of having friends who will come over at 10:00 p.m. to bathe my skunked dog.

We arrived home hours later to a clean dog, completely ruined rugs, a still-standing house, and a bottle of isopropyl alcohol, 99 percent flammable, sitting on the counter beside the stove. The bottle looked exactly like the white vinegar bottle, and for some reason it was in the cabinet where we keep our vinegars and oils. I never thought twice when I grabbed it and poured it into the pot.

Over the next few days, friends and neighbors stopped by to check on us and drop off meals. I've been in the church most of my life and been a part of innumerable "meal trains" for new moms and post-accident families where the word goes out and their fellow Christians show up bearing casseroles.

It's beautiful when it happens, and I've been the recipient of it a time or two. But I've never been a part of a community that doesn't organize a meal train, that doesn't have a central line of communication, that doesn't have anything in common except we live in the same town and they know who we are and what happened.

One neighbor—an outspoken liberal with yard signs and demanding social media posts—brought over a grocery bag full of meals and cookies. Another neighbor who for years had a Confederate flag hanging on the porch dropped off chicken soup. A friend from across town and her girlfriend made us two meals with more food than we could handle. Another neighbor heard what happened and dropped off filet mignon; she didn't even know us. A dear friend and his boyfriend came for dinner just to be with us. Another friend who had hardly spoken to us since the pandemic and election texted that she'd be over with some cherry cobbler. Yet another pulled into our driveway bearing pots of plants she'd dug up to give me to transplant and instead dug through my garden and transplanted them herself.

What an embarrassment of riches. What a cornucopia of community. None of these people were our best friends, those with whom we felt deep kinship and intimacy. They were just ordinary people in an ordinary community moved by ordinary care for other humans in a moment of need—despite the fact that some might view their political views, lifestyle, church, or beliefs as incompatible with neighborliness. I

found the flag reprehensible and the yard signs less than logi-
cal, but the person standing in front of me offering a meal
or a helping hand? It's nearly impossible to demonize them.

I hadn't meant to become so isolated, stuck with those
who were mostly just like me, but this was the first time I
had such an array of people in my life—really different and
distinct people, people who would disagree vehemently with
one another. For a long time, I'd felt afraid to be with those
who weren't like me, afraid I'd veer off into beliefs or practices that would dishonor God. But the opposite happened.
The more unstuck from my echo chambers and groupthink
environments I became, the less I felt the need for approval
from pastors and leaders and other Christian gatekeepers,
the more spacious my heart became, and the more I just
wanted to be a person who loved Jesus and let the rest of it
work itself out.

All these neighbors and friends know we're Christians,
and many of them have seen a side of Christianity over the
last several years that has turned them off forever. Some of
them are atheists or agnostics or Unitarian Universalists or
Muslim. Some of them are ex-evangelicals, and some go to
church with us on Sunday. Some have voted the same way
for sixty years; others are still figuring things out. Some of
them are gay, and some of them are dyed-in-the-wool Presbyterian. Some are feminists, and some are hippies. One is
a conservative homeschool mom, and another just marched
in a Pride parade with her girlfriend.

There is something about regular proximity with those who aren't just like us that softens our hearts and helps us shed the self-protective shells we wear. We don't become like them, but we learn to see them more fully in all their complexity.

It's hard to hide when you're in need. And it's even harder to hate the ones who show up to help.

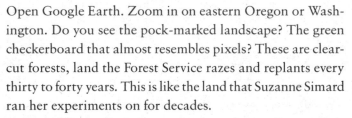

Open Google Earth. Zoom in on eastern Oregon or Washington. Do you see the pock-marked landscape? The green checkerboard that almost resembles pixels? These are clear-cut forests, land the Forest Service razes and replants every thirty to forty years. This is like the land that Suzanne Simard ran her experiments on for decades.

Simard freely admits that we're dependent on the wood we get from the logging industry, but she's also convinced that clear-cutting forests—and all the chemicals needed to rid the forests of "trash trees" like aspen, birch, and alder—is not the sustainable route forward. Eco-philosopher (and somewhat of an anarchist) Derrick Jensen says, "How you perceive the world affects how you behave in the world. There's a great line by a Canadian lumberman who said, 'When I look at trees, I see dollar bills,' and if you look at trees and see dollar bills you'll treat them one way, and if you look at trees and see trees, you'll treat them another way."[5] Despite the money to be made from these rapidly grown pine and fir plots, Simard looked at trees and saw not only the trees but also all the things that were going on beneath the trees. She wondered, *Is there a better, more sustainable, less chemically dependent, more long-term-benefit way to take only what we absolutely need and nothing more and have healthier forests too?*

In the past, the Forest Service and logging industry thought that different species of trees competed with one another. They believed that only by planting like with like could they get a robust harvest of trees. They believed it would be an "evolutionary paradox"[6] for trees (particularly trees of different kinds) to not only cooperate with one another but also support and nourish one another. Simard's research changed everything— once the Forest Service finally listened to her. She writes, "Pine got nitrogen from alder, not through the soil but thanks to mycorrhizal fungi. And those alder were sending vitamins to pine directly through a pipeline. . . . Far from birch being the 'demon weed,' it was generously giving fir resources."[7]

After two decades of planting, watching, testing, and waiting, Simard and her team saw that "firs performed better in the neighborhood of birches than where . . . they'd grown only among other firs. They had better nutrition—the birch leaves building the soil—and less *Armillaria* root disease, the bacteria along the birch roots providing a bundle of nitrogen and immunity with a potent mix of antibiotics and other inhibitory compounds. *Grown intimately together*, this forest had almost twice the productivity of the stands we'd trenched between the species two decades earlier."[8] This underground network of nearly microscopic fungi was the cargo train carrying everything the trees needed to one another.

Poet W. H. Auden once wrote, "A culture is no better than its woods,"[9] and if we are like the woods of a homogenous pine plantation, our culture is doomed to fail. We simply cannot grow strong and tall and resilient only among our own. We need diversity, not just for diversity's sake but because we are, like the trees of the forest, mutualists. We cannot get what we need only from our own kind, those who think like us, act like us, vote like us, and plan like us. Nor can we truly give to only our own kind. This would be like bringing oranges to a party hosted by an orange grower. The orange grower doesn't *need* our oranges, and so the gift isn't really a gift; it's surplus. But when we mingle with and serve those who are not like us, we set a better feast before one another, a diverse, nutrient-rich, complex feast.

When the wildfire smoke clears, I take to the trails again, this time to one aptly called Pine Trail. The path is littered with fallen, rust-colored needles, a soft bed for my feet as I walk whisper-quiet through the woods. This is a place we snowshoe in the winter, but I rarely come here in the summer. I needed a slow hike today though, something quiet and calm.

It rained yesterday, thank God, and droplets are still fluttering down through the trees. It is strangely silent, hardly any birdsong. Above me the pines tower, like an ancient cathedral whose roof has fallen, the gaps letting bits of light filter through to the path. The understory isn't thick here, but the forest is in the process of being rewilded by the caretakers of this park. Seventy years ago, part of it was logged and then a small wildfire broke out in another part, burning a few hundred acres before it could be contained. After that, the state took over the land and has been restoring it ever since.

Rewilding a place is no easy task. It is long, arduous, and not for one who wants quick results, or even results in their lifetime. Robin Wall Kimmerer writes, "Restoring land without restoring relationship is an empty exercise."[10] Rewilding is about relationships, relationships between trees and soil and mycelia and nurse logs and the understory. When Tree 103 fell, it was due to natural causes, and she will remain there as nutrients for future generations of trees, feeding them for far longer than she stood tall and strong and resilient. But when a large disturbance happens, from wind, burning, or clear-cutting, something of this magnitude takes considerable time to heal. And although the damage might appear to be primarily above the ground, what is happening below the ground is what will help the forest heal.

Jon Luoma wrote about a scientist who was convinced that "mycorrhizal fungi are keys to how a damaged below ground ecosystem in the forest—and then the forest itself—heals,"[11] and he was on to something. By the time Simard's data was in a few years later, she was able to say definitively that "the seedlings . . . were regenerating in the network of the old trees."[12] Even though a forest may appear to be completely cut down, destroyed, burned, ruined, there is still a beautiful, networked communion happening beneath the ground.

Beneath my feet, as I walk on this needle-laden path, in less than one square foot there are thousands of *miles* of mycelia. Lyanda Lynn Haupt calls mycelia "an eternal matrix woven through the soil."[13] And all those miles of mycelia are sharing information, food and nutrients, carbon and nitrogen, hormones and water, phosphorus and warning signals with the trees and plants above them. Absolutely unselfishly, they are connecting different species with one another to facilitate growth, and there is a flourishing they could not otherwise sustain on their own.

If we want to be a flourishing community and world, we must learn to be mutualists, giving and receiving as there is need, intent on building resilient and regenerative communities alongside those who are not like us, not even a little bit. We cannot be isolated. We will not flourish as a forest of individual trees who stand alone—us against the world. We will either burn down or grow spindly and impoverished. We are, every one of us, connected in ways that may surprise or shock us.

At the top of a hill overlooking a small beaver pond and meadow, I find a bench made from fallen branches, and I sit for a while. I think of Elizabeth Barrett Browning's famous lines,

Earth's crammed with heaven,
and every common bush afire with God,
but only he who sees takes off his shoes;
the rest sit round and pluck blackberries.[14]

I want to be one who sees the beauty of heaven on earth and not just the hell we've made of it. It does feel like hell sometimes, I can't lie. There have been days and weeks and months and moments over the past several years when I couldn't believe I was a citizen of this country, and we are all making such awful decisions about how to live and treat one another. But the truth is beneath my feet.

Mycorrhizal fungi show me earth as it is in heaven: mutualism, generosity, neighborliness, decreasing so even sometimes my enemies increase, selflessness, even a kind of love. Their work below ground creates a resilient, complex ecosystem with the roots of trees and plants that mix and mingle as neighbors in nutrient-rich soil and a mosaic of decomposition teeming with death and life. Those mycelia, as unimpressive as they seem at first sight, are the restorative agent, the hardest working of them all. Sitting here, I see the fruit of their labor, firs and birches, aspens and beeches, black walnuts and pines—the forest is crammed with them, thick and rich and wildly diverse.

It's heaven here.

10

HERE IS MOVEMENT

FOREST

For we know that if the earthly tent we live in is destroyed, we have a building from God, an eternal house in heaven, not built by human hands.

—2 Corinthians 5:1

God owns heaven, but He craves the earth.
—Anne Sexton, "The Earth"

I have spent nearly my entire life moving. Recently, I had reason to list all the home addresses at which I'd lived as an adult. Between the ages of twenty and forty-two, I'd stepped across the threshold of twenty-seven doors and called myself home. On the list were apartments and dorms, small bungalows where my roommates and I slept four to a room, and bigger suburban homes where we each had a room to call our own. I've roomed with families, worked as a resident assistant in college, bunked down in wilderness camps for the summer, and spent six months living overseas with a friend. I have lived in eleven states. Since marrying, Nate and I have moved cross-country four times and bought and sold four houses.

Maybe this kind of transience is normal in some cultures, but I have friends who have never moved from their hometown or the state of their birth, and the thought of leaving the roots they've put down either terrifies them or never occurs to them. I am grateful for the expanse upon which I've rambled. What I lack in roots I hope I make up for in a breadth of experiences and relationships.

But I cannot deny the desire deep within me for roots, for a single home to return to each holiday, for a hometown where even just one of my family members still lives. Nowhere is home, by which I suppose I could say that everywhere is home.

Coming back to this place that is as close to a hometown as I can get—as it is the last place my family lived intact, even if the fractures were beginning to show—feels like a vestige of hope. There is the desire that even though we lack children we can still sink ourselves into this home, this land, this community and leave a little something behind us. I don't know if there will be anyone who cares that we are gone when we have gone, but I know I have planted a few trees that the beavers have yet to salvage for their own. I know after three years of pestering (added to the pesters of thirty years of residents before us) we have convinced the township to fix the dysfunctional storm overflow in our front yard. I know we have renovated and restored our home from its derelict state. I know we have kept an eye on our elderly neighbors' house when they have left and given them a key when we have left ours. I know we are members at our local co-op and patrons at our local library, where they know our names. We have a line of credit at our local coffeehouse. I know our names are known when we buy paint at the local hardware store or order a pizza or pledge a sum of money to a local nonprofit's fundraiser.

Are these roots? I don't know. But they must be at least the tendrils of them.

One might think the Adirondacks are all green space, blue lakes, and tiny vacation hamlets or derelict old villages inhabited by year-round locals who will never thrive off the tourist economy. But down inconspicuous dirt roads or behind wrought-iron gates or sometimes advertised with tasteful signs nearly blending into the environment are the Great Camps. These are owned by the Rockefellers and Guggenheims and Carnegies, on land once camped on by Roosevelts and Emerson and Edison.

The Great Camps were mostly built in the Arts and Crafts tradition—big, bold, and blocky porches with reds, greens, browns, and mustard-yellow painted trims. They are an earthy opulence, with beds covered with Pendleton wools, thick Persian carpets on the floors surrounded by log-hewn walls, headboards and furniture crafted from white birch saplings and knotty ancient pines. There are no short-ages of moose heads and stuffed loons, lumberjack plaids and woven baskets made by local Indigenous people. One former Great Camp now offers a luxury camping experience to the tune of $3,500 a night. They are booked through next year.

In the gilded age, New York City's rich and famous would leave the city of elites and begin a seasonal caravan through Rhode Island, the Berkshires in western Massachusetts, and the Adirondacks. They owned grand homes in each that they would fill with climbing socialites thirsty for this new money lifestyle. Homeowners and guests would stay at these houses for a night or a week and then move on to the next, a kind of extravagant homelessness.

It seems that no matter where we are, we would rather not be there.

On the road between Saranac and Tupper Lakes, there is a small pull-off with a telltale Adirondack brown and yellow sign. Ampersand Mountain is not one of the Adirondack High Peaks, but it is a popular hiking spot. The first mile is an easy walk; the second mile is a difficult hike up rock scrambles and steep grades. The summit offers one of the best views in the eastern region, with mountain peaks in every direction and an overlook of the gorgeous, privately owned Ampersand Lake—where, if one knows where to look, one can see the Rockefeller houses and grounds.

I have no interest in seeing the summit views or the houses and grounds today. The first twenty minutes of the trek is through old-growth forest, and this is where I will be spending the next few hours.

I am not going for a hike, and I don't even know if it can be said I'm going for a walk. I am going *to* walk, yes, but not *for* a walk. The walk is not the point. M. Amos Clifford, in his book *Your Guide to Forest Bathing*, says of this kind of exercise, "The destination . . . is 'here' not 'there.'"[1] And so I am going here, not there, wherever *here* is.

It is often said that environmentalist and conservation advocate John Muir hated the word *hiking* and preferred the word *sauntering*. From a conversation between them, Albert Palmer records Muir as saying, "I don't like either the word or the thing. People ought to saunter in the mountains, not hike!"[2] Muir follows up the comment with an etymological explanation of the word *saunter*, which, as best as I can find, comes from Thoreau's famous essay "Walking." Thoreau himself probably learned it from Samuel Johnson's dictionary definition of the word from 1755.

I myself prefer Thoreau's phrasing best. He wrote that saunter is "beautifully derived 'from idle people who roved about the country, in the Middle Ages, and asked charity, under pretense of going *à la Sainte Terre,*' to the Holy Land, till the children exclaimed, 'There goes a Sainte-Terrer,' a *Saunterer,* a Holy-Lander. They who never go to the Holy Land in their walks, as they pretend, are indeed mere idlers and vagabonds; but they who do go there are saunterers in the good sense, such as I mean." Thoreau goes on, though, adding to Johnson's definition, to say that some might say that *saunter* is derived from the Latin *sans terre,* "without land or home," which might mean having no particular home or, in a sense, being at home everywhere.[3]

Which is it? I don't know, but I rather like both.

I park my car and stash my water bottle and small nature journal in my day pack. I tuck my pant legs into my socks—less a fashion statement and more a defense against the Lyme-ridden ticks that are becoming more common in this part of the country—and cross the threshold into the green haven.

I am here to saunter, to move, to stay still, to wander, to idle, to rest, to be at home. I am here not to judge where I am but to receive it, such as it is, as the gift that it is. I am here not to make a home in this forest or this place or this moment or even this me but simply to be where I am as I am, to be at home in my own self and in the Spirit, who is also in me.

It is said that St. Augustine coined the phrase *solvitur ambulando*, meaning "it is solved by walking." Today I endeavor not to solve or resolve but simply to move from here to here to here. My endeavor, at its basest, is honesty, to notice what I notice and not pretend to notice more or less. To receive what I receive and not make up what I want to receive or what others have received before me. It is to live in the truth of this moment.

I have felt more shame than I know how to hold for my transience, for my lack of roots and rootedness in both places and ideas. Even if no one ever said it aloud to me, I feel the judgment that comes when I move to yet another home, or change a perspective, or learn and shift and grow out from a place where others knew me once, or die to a certain way of being or becoming or belonging. I question sometimes whether I am trying to escape. I scorn myself for it, but then I remember a poet's words: "Why should a man be scorned, if finding himself in prison, he tries to get out and go home?"[4]

Can we be imprisoned by ideals and communities, churches and friends, leaders and institutions? Can we grow out of them or away from them? Can we say to ourselves and others, "This is not the most important thing in my world anymore; it is not the space in which I can grow anymore" without demonizing them or them demonizing us?

I wonder why we find it so uncomfortable to maintain relationships with those who have sauntered to goodness elsewhere and found it. I wonder why we feel we must be the ones who grab on to them and hold them back, what we think it says about us when they move away from where we are. I once heard Duke theology professor Norman Wirzba say that our work as Christians is to "liberate others into wholeness," and I have never forgotten that. I wonder if some of us might blanche at words like those because we're afraid that one's liberation into wholeness says something about the space they leave behind in our own lives when they leave. But another's wholeness doesn't have to mean our brokenness. There is room enough in this world for everyone to become whole.

On the surface, I envy my friends with roots and rootedness, those who have never left the cocoon of their family and hometown and geographic culture, or their faith tradition and way of life. But beneath that sliver of green, I don't envy it at all. The truth is that, despite my attempts to root and find and make and stay in a home, I am not sure God made me that way. I have always been looking for new horizons and new places to explore or inhabit, despite the evangelical obsession with staying still and digging in.

The tension with which I wrestle here is not especially particular or even special. It is a feeling of being out of place, lacking, missing something essential. There is a German word, *Sehnsucht*, which means a longing for a place or experience. The Portuguese have a word for this too: *saudade*. The Welsh use *hiraeth*. Perhaps the closest we come to it in English is *nostalgia*, but nostalgia conjures up images of longing for the past, while all the rest of these words convey a longing for that which has not yet come. This is how I feel about most of life. I do not look behind me and long for any of it, not anymore. But deep within me there is an unshakeable, steady hope for something completely new that works in ways the old never has.

Perhaps that is what the New Testament Christians would have called *elpis*, "to anticipate and welcome."

I am growing even more sure—despite what years of apologetics and local churches and dogmatic doctrines have told me—that this desire for change doesn't make me wrong. It is not always the moral choice to stay and the immoral choice to leave. What is the moral choice for one may indeed be the immoral choice for another. This is a difficult tension to live with, but live with it we must.

Solvitur ambulando. It is solved by walking.

We do not grow by staying exactly the same.

And others do not grow by keeping us always with them, exactly as we and they always were.

In Chaim Potok's second book about his fictional protagonist Asher Lev, Asher says, "When I paint, I think of the truth of the painting. I try never to think of the consequences."[5] I am not sure we all have the luxury of not thinking about the consequences of our art and life and faith— and whether we think about them or not doesn't negate the existence of them. Everything we do and leave undone has a consequence. Every point of doctrine, every vote, every face we have beheld, and every human and their story we have ignored it all matters. But I understand Asher's sentiment that we cannot think too hard about the consequences while at the same time making the best of whatever it is we've been called to make.

On my drive to the mountains today, I am talking with a faraway friend who is working through a book idea, offers from publishers, and a suggestion from his editor to write about a conflict he navigated. His book idea is beautiful, and I champion it, but his consternation about the consequences of publishing with this publisher or that one, for this amount of money or that one, this kind of book or another kind is going to eat him alive. I tell him this and chase it up with the admission that his wrestling is not uncommon. I've gotten lost in those weeds myself a time or two while writing this very book. Of course I want this book to sell well and reach many people; it would be disingenuous for me to say otherwise. But if I had let that aim be my master, I would have written a terrible book, and you, reader, would be wise to toss a book like that in the garbage. If, however, my aim is to tell the truth and tell it well, then consequences be damned— I can't control them anyway.

This is the work of humans, to be fruitful, to inhabit, to take up space, to live long and die well, to feed the generations to come. Our whole work as humans is to be "liberated into wholeness," and wholeness means not simply that we are a new creature in a new creation but that consequences are not the driving factor of our actions any longer. The driving force of our actions is delighting in and moving toward all that is true, good, and beautiful. That's it.

Asher's line resonates with me because I think I have lived for too long with a foreboding sense of the weightiness of everything on me. It is not so much that I have wanted to do right or be perfect but that I have believed that my actions or inactions matter more than they do. I am convinced now that if Jesus is true and good, then he is more interested in being *with* me as I am than in watching me perform or practice to be something I am not. Jesus is interested in the here and now, which is why he was able to weep in a garden and beg the cup be taken from him. I'm not sure the tears would have come if the only thing in his mind and heart was the consequences.

Behold, he was right there.

Behold, he was sad and afraid and maybe angry, grieved, and a little uncertain.

Behold, he was right where he was in that moment and nothing more or less.

"God, make me more like that," I pray these days.

I write my name, phone number, and the time I'm beginning my saunter in the trail book and notice I'm only the second person here today. The mosquitos are biting, and I pull my sweatshirt hood up around my baseball cap and my sleeves down past my wrists. So much for wanting to find a mossy rock to sit on and think. I'll be breakfast, lunch, and dinner for these critters if I stop for longer than twenty seconds.

The sounds of the road fade away behind me, and soon the sound of a brook cascading down boulders is all I hear. As I draw nearer, I can see the moss is an inch thick on the rocks and four inches thick on all the fallen beech trees. This forest is full of beech trees, and everywhere I look there are buttresses standing strong, their nurse logs long gone. I could fit my whole body beneath one. Along the wide path are tiny balsam firs all dotted with bright, almost florescent green tips, the sure sign of new growth from old growth. I pinch off a few—careful not to take more than one from each tree—to make a tea when I get home. I think of the closing lines of

Philip Larkin's poem "The Trees": "Last year is dead," now it is time start "afresh, afresh, afresh."[6]

Start afresh, I wonder to myself. Can we do that? Are we capable of doing that as a culture and a society that are as fractured as ours is right now? Are we too critical of those who leave or of those who stay? Or are we too much like another poet's poem about trees: "All felled, felled, are all felled"?[7]

One fallen log is slumped over another in an undulating form, so decomposed it looks like a sleeping giant nestled into his bed. Opportunist ferns sprout from every nook and cranny, mushrooms, fungi, lichen, and moss their backdrop. The ground beneath the giant is loamy, and I pull away a few brown leaves from where he lays. A thick web of mycelia is revealed, working just as hard as the sleeping giant above, even if to the naked eye they both have the appearance of absolute stillness, even death. I remember the forestry professor's words about Tree 103: "Dead, yes, but I prefer to think that [she's] just not vertical anymore."[8] There, towering above this reclining giant, is another giant, strong and sure, being fruitful and multiplying, but even he will not last forever. He will fall, probably sometime sooner than we'd all like, and there he will lie just as the giant below him lies now. This is the way of life, and not just the forest life. It is the way of our human lives too. Despite all our hope in a world to come and belief in a new earth, the earth we live within now is foreshadowing the way we will all go.

This may sound defeatist. My hope is you didn't pick up

this book to read of easy solutions and principles for keeping your way of life intact. We cannot keep our way of life. We cannot guarantee the consequences. We cannot control the outcomes. And I am certain, more than I ever have been before, that the more we try to control the "wild and precious life" we live, the more damage we will do to all of us. Poet Rainer Maria Rilke writes, "Earth! Invisible! / What, if not change, is your desperate mission?"[9] What indeed?

What if the miracle of living this life is not that we all get our way but that we sink our roots and souls and bodies deeper and deeper into the place God has put us, for just the time God has put us there? This place is not even a physical place—remember, there is no moral good or evil to leaving or staying—but simply the space we inhabit today. *Adsum*. What if the miracle of life is that we move through belief and unbelief, doubt and faith, joy and sorrow, anger and grief, truth and faith, being as wholly ourselves as we can be in that moment? Is being here, wherever here is, wholeness?

I think it is.

I am trying to find my way home on this earth again.

I am trying to change by degrees and make space for those who walk beside me to change by degrees too. I am interested in liberation into wholeness. Madeleine L'Engle once wrote, "The coming of the Kingdom is creation coming to be what it was meant to be."[10] This is the home I'm after. An unshakable kingdom full of malleable creatures in a morphing and growing and expanding creation becoming liberated. I am trying to find a new way of being and belonging and becoming in this world while still valuing the places and people I have left behind. I want to thank them for what they have given me and grieve for what they have broken in me and find healing and resilience among them but not of them.

"Things fall apart," William Butler Yeats wrote, "mere anarchy is loosed upon the world."[11] Fall apart indeed. I find the somewhat trustworthy terrain of the church and the world and politics and our health all fallen apart and anarchy in my soul.

It is not a new home I seek though; it is the one home I have had all along.

I cannot be at home, "at peace and in place," if I find my identity in a belief or practice, political party or church. I cannot be at peace and in place if I craft my work and words to mere men and women instead of to the God who made us all. I cannot be at peace and in place if I despise my neighbor when they vote differently from me or despise myself for staying in broken systems for far too long. To be at home means to acknowledge all the complexity of who I am and who God is and who my neighbor is and to receive it all as the gift it is. It is to say to the broken reflection staring back at me, "I am becoming whole." It is to say to the person I hate, "You are becoming whole." It is to say to the ones who have hurt me and the ones who haunt me, "You are becoming whole, and it is a wonder to behold." To be at peace and in place is to be at peace with paradox, with the inside-out and upside-down sense of wonder and ache at the same time. This feels nearly impossible, but this is the work of a Christian in the world. To say, "I am here, and I am not yet all here." "I am complete, and I am a work in process." "I am dying, and I am living." "I know the answer, and I know nothing."

Due north in the valley below Ampersand Mountain, near a marshy bog on the outskirts of Lower Saranac Lake, there is an eastern white pine. I do not know her name. Perhaps she is a sister to Tree 103. Perhaps the same bird or gust of wind that carried the gauzy-winged seed that became Tree 103 carried another seed to the valley, and perhaps that seed sprouted and became this towering pine. They are of similar age. It's not too difficult to believe.

On his thirtieth birthday, a local ecologist, Eric Danielson, leads a small group of people on a five-hour bushwhack to the north edge of an esker in the Ampersand valley.[12] Howard Stoner, the mathematician who first measured Tree 103 as the tallest in New York State, is with him. They had seen the crown of this pine billowing out around other trees from the bird's-eye view on a satellite map and have come to measure her.

Hours later, they reach her, and she measures 13.6 feet around, not impressive by redwood or sequoia standards, but she towers through the canopy so high that they can't see her top branches. Danielson pulls out his hypsometer, a device used to measure trees, and scans the pine.

She is taller than the Brooklyn Bridge, taller than the now-fallen Tree 103. She is the tallest tree in New York State. She mothers the trees around her in this valley, shelters the understory beneath her, and is nourished by and nourishes the forest floor around her. She is what she is and will be until she is no longer recognizable as a tree at all. I wonder if her root system shook when, a few miles away, her sister fell last year.

I love Tree 103, but I am not like Tree 103. Maybe someday I will be, fallen and still on the forest floor, nursing generations to come. I am not even like this other tall tree in the Ampersand basin, though I might aspire to be.

I am a tiny sapling on the floor of this forest, sinking my tendrils down into a nurse log who has given herself for me. I am receiving nutrients from fellow trees of different species. I am a fern unfurling. I am the tip of a balsam bough, green and fresh, new to this world. I am a white trillium, here today, gone tomorrow. I am lichen, clinging to something solid for as long as I can. I am the soft, dark earth, the composition of death. I am the soil, moving and making space for life to flourish. I am living on land that doesn't belong to me and never will. I am stardust and clay and bone. I am the whole forest. I come from dust and to dust I will return. I am temporal, and I am eternal, and neither makes complete sense, but I believe it nonetheless. *Adsum*. I am here.

ACKNOWLEDGMENTS

Books are often written in solitude, but they are almost never written alone. This book was written at a desk piled high with works by Wendell Berry, Madeleine L'Engle, Mary Oliver, Rachel Carson, Peter Wohlleben, Robin Wall Kimmerer, Suzanne Simard, and more. If there is anything good in this work, it was born from their minds first. I am indebted to each of them—particularly Robin Wall Kimmerer, who loves the same Adirondacks I do and has spent her life studying and honoring them with her students and family.

Thank you to Katelyn Beaty for trusting me when I said, "I want to write this book, but I want to write it without an outline, proposal, or signed contract. Will you let me?" I know that was a risk, and I'm deeply grateful for an editor who trusted me enough to let me try. I think this is a better book for it, and I know I am a better writer for the freedom it afforded me.

I also thank John Blase, my friend and literary agent, who pushed me to go for it when I said I couldn't write this book with an outline already written out. Who trusted "the woods in me" when I was kept from going to the woods. Who talked me off more than one cliff when crippling anxiety took hold. You help me be brave, John, when I am so very not.

Thank you, Cohort Six (especially Monica, Kristin, Hailey, Jen, Brandon, Terry, Trish, Greg, and Joe). This book was written alongside our years together, and you have all formed me in ways I still can't estimate. Thank you for keeping Jesus at the center.

I'm thankful to my little group of writers, the Cairns, Jess Herberger, Sara Billups, and Amber Haines. This will be the sixth book that's been birthed between us since we began meeting together for encouragement and prayer and a kind of belief in one another I've never experienced in a group of writers before. I love you all.

Thank you to Silver Bay YMCA for giving me a week to write in the Adirondacks. Thank you to Laity Lodge for giving me so much even when I couldn't take you up on it. Thank you to the Wild Center for the beautiful magic of Forest Music and the work you've done for our local community. Thank you to the Adirondack Experience for preserving and promoting what is most beautiful around here. Thank you to Paul Smith's College for the VIC and for taking care of so much Adirondack land. Thank you to the *Adirondack Life* magazine for lighting the spark that became this book.

Thank you to my readers on lorewilbert.com. Honestly. I don't even know what to say. You are the reason I'm doing this, the only reason I can, and the reason I want to keep doing it for the rest of my life. Thank you especially to Melissa A., Jess H., Tiffany R., Renee B., Lindsay T., JMM, M. Takatsuki, P. Wessner, Lolly Gator, D. Erwin, Marcia D., Drew R., Charlotte L., Candy L., Lesley A., Jenny P., Steve B., J. Hughes, Elizabeth J., Selena C., David Y., Rachel G., Sara W., and the Thompsons. Your support means the world to me.

Thank you to my fellow writers and colaborers. Even though we may not talk often, I see the work you are doing in the world and it matters: Sarah Westfall, Karen Prior, David Taylor, Seth Haines, Sharon Miller, Aarik Danielsen, Ashley Hales, Jen Michel, Shawn Smucker, Amanda Opelt, and so many more.

Thank you, Mom, for letting me be a little wild.

Thank you, Steve, for being my friend.

Thank you, Sole, for being faithful.

Thank you, Philip, just for everything.

Thank you to my Bean, my favorite forest adventurer, my favorite everything, my compass and my kin. You have made me be more like the person I want to be, and you push me to be even more than that. Thank you for your patience and your love and for bearing with me in all these iterations of life.

Thank you to my love, Nathan. I read every one of these chapters aloud to you. Some you cried at the end of, some you said were good, some you just said, "Good job, baby," by which you meant "You're not there yet, keep pushing." But more than all of it, you listened and you listen. You have listened to me process years of grief this past decade and never told me to shut up or shut down. You make space for people as they are, and you have made space for me to become what I am becoming. You are kind when I am short. You are long-suffering when I am hyper-focused. You are a servant when I can't see straight.

Finally, thank you to our neighbors and community. I am so glad to be your neighbor.

RECOMMENDED READING

Berry, Wendell. (All of the Port Williams series.)

———. *The Art of the Commonplace*. New York: Catapult, 2018.

———. *This Day: Sabbath Poems Collected and New, 1979–2013*. Berkeley: Counterpoint, 2013.

———. *The Unsettling of America: Culture and Agriculture*. Berkeley: Counterpoint, 2015.

Brueggemann, Walter. *The Land: Place as Gift, Promise, and Challenge in Biblical Faith*. 2nd ed. Overtures to Biblical Theology. Minneapolis: Fortress, 2002.

Carson, Rachel. *Silent Spring*. Fortieth anniversary edition. New York: Houghton Mifflin, 2002.

Haupt, Lyanda Lynn. *Rooted: Life at the Crossroads of Science, Nature, and Spirit*. Boston: Little, Brown, 2022.

Kimmerer, Robin Wall. *Braiding Sweetgrass: Indigenous Wisdom, Scientific Knowledge, and the Teachings of Plants*. Minneapolis: Milkweed, 2013.

———. *Gathering Moss: A Natural and Cultural History of Mosses*. Corvallis: Oregon State University Press, 2003.

L'Engle, Madeleine. *The Irrational Season*. San Francisco: HarperSanFrancisco, 1995.

Luoma, Jon R. *The Hidden Forest: The Biography of an Ecosystem*. Corvallis: Oregon State University Press, 2006.

Macfarlane, Robert. *Underland: A Deep Time Journey*. New York: Norton, 2019.

Maloof, Joan. *Teaching the Trees: Lessons from the Forest*. Athens: University of Georgia Press, 2007.

O'Donohue, John. *To Bless the Space Between Us: A Book of Blessings*. New York: Doubleday, 2008.

Oliver, Mary. *Upstream: Selected Essays*. New York: Penguin, 2016.

Pollan, Michael. *Second Nature: A Gardener's Education*. New York: Grove, 2018.

Powers, Richard. *The Overstory*. New York: Norton, 2018.

Rilke, Rainer Maria. *Rilke's Book of Hours: Love Poems to God*. Translated by Anita Barrows and Joanna Macy. New York: Riverhead, 2005.

Sharkey, Erin, ed. *A Darker Wilderness: Black Nature Writing from Soil to Stars*. Minneapolis: Milkweed, 2023.

Sheldrake, Merlin. *Entangled Life: How Fungi Make Our Worlds, Change Our Minds, and Shape Our Futures*. New York: Random House, 2020.

Simard, Suzanne. *Finding the Mother Tree: Discovering the Wisdom of the Forest*. New York: Knopf, 2021.

Sleeth, Matthew. *Reforesting Faith: What Trees Teach Us about the Nature of God and His Love for Us*. New York: Waterbrook, 2019.

Solnit, Rebecca. *Wanderlust: A History of Walking*. New York: Viking, 2000.

Williams, Terry Tempest. *Erosion: Essays of Undoing*. New York: Pantheon, 1994.

————. *The Hour of Land: A Personal Topography of America's National Parks*. New York: Sarah Crichton Books / Farrar, Straus, and Giroux, 2016.

Wirzba, Norman, and Fred Bahnson. *Making Peace with the Land: God's Call to Reconcile with Creation*. Downers Grove, IL: IVP Books, 2012.

Wohlleben, Peter. *The Hidden Life of Trees: What They Feel, How They Communicate—Discoveries from a Secret World*. Glasgow, UK: William Collins, 2017.

NOTES

Chapter 1 Here Is Loss: Invitation

1. Waskiewicz's comment can be found in Susan Orlean, "The Tallest Known Tree in New York Falls in the Forest," *New Yorker*, January 18, 2022, https://www.newyorker.com/news/afterword/the-tallest-known-tree-in-new-york-falls-in-the-forest.

2. "Water Quality: Protecting the Waters of the Adirondack Park," Adirondack Council, accessed September 27, 2023, https://www.adirondackcouncil.org/page/water-quality-89.html.

3. Orlean, "Tallest Known Tree."

4. Other sources say *Adirondack* was derived from an Iroquois word, *rontaks*, for the Algonquins who ate tree bark.

5. Emily Dickinson, "Tell All the Truth but Tell It Slant," Poetry Foundation, https://www.poetryfoundation.org/poems/56824/tell-all-the-truth-but-tell-it-slant-1263.

6. Anne LaMott (@ANNELAMOTT), "You own everything that happened to you. Tell your stories. If people wanted you to write warmly about them, they should have behaved better." X (formerly Twitter), April 23, 2012, 8:16 p.m., https://twitter.com/ANNELAMOTT/status/194580559962439681?lang=en.

7. Chaim Potok, *My Name Is Asher Lev* (New York: Fawcett, 1975), 368 (emphasis added).

8. James Galvin, "Limber Pines," in *Poems about Trees*, ed. Harry Thomas (New York: Knopf, 2019), 70.

9. See Lore Wilbert, "The Hiddenness of Goodness or the Goodness of Hiddenness," Sayable, March 16, 2022, https://www.sayable.net/blog/2022/3/16/the-hiddenness-of-goodness-or-the-goodness-of-hiddenness.

10. Thomas Merton, "Hagia Sophia," in *A Thomas Merton Reader*, ed. Thomas P. McDonnell (New York: Image/Doubleday, 1989), 506.

11. Douglas Wood, *Fawn Island* (Minneapolis: University of Minnesota Press, 2001), 3–4.

12. Wendell Berry, *A Timbered Choir: The Sabbath Poems, 1979–1997* (New York: Counterpoint, 1999), 178.

13. Jon R. Luoma, *The Hidden Forest: The Biography of an Ecosystem* (Corvallis: Oregon State University Press, 2006), 72.

14. Mary Oliver, *Upstream: Selected Essays* (New York: Penguin Books, 2016), 154.

15. Robin Wall Kimmerer, *Gathering Moss: A Natural and Cultural History of Mosses* (Corvallis: Oregon State University Press, 2003), 36.

16. William Carlos Williams, "Burning the Christmas Greens," in Thomas, *Poems about Trees*, 144.

17. Madeleine L'Engle, *The Irrational Season* (San Francisco: HarperSanFrancisco, 1995), 201.

18. Robin Wall Kimmerer says that other species "are recognized not only as persons, but also as teachers who can inspire how we might live." Kimmerer, "Nature Needs a New Pronoun: To Stop the Age of Extinction, Let's Start by Ditching 'It,'" *Yes!*, March 30, 2015, https://www.yesmagazine.org/issue/together-earth/2015/03/30/alternative-grammar-a-new-language-of-kinship.

Chapter 2 Here Is Here: Space

1. Christina Rossetti, "In the Bleak Midwinter," first published in the 1872 issue of *Scribner's Monthly*, available at https://www.poetryfoundation.org/poems/53216/in-the-bleak-midwinter.

2. Tim Suttle, *Shrink: Faithful Ministry in a Church-Growth Culture* (Grand Rapids: Zondervan, 2014), 30.

3. John Piper released a book titled *Don't Waste Your Life* (Wheaton: Crossway) in 2003 that became a bestseller.

4. Mary Oliver, *Upstream: Selected Essays* (New York: Penguin Books, 2016), 28.

5. Richard Wilbur, "Love Calls Us to the Things of This World," in *Collected Poems: 1943–2004* (New York: Houghton Mifflin Harcourt, 2004), 307. The title of the poem is a play on 1 John 2:15.

6. David Wagoner, "Lost," *Poetry*, July 1971, Poetry Foundation, https://www.poetryfoundation.org/poetrymagazine/browse?contentId=31968.

7. Scott Cairns, *Slow Pilgrim: Collected Poems* (Brewster, MA: Paraclete, 2015), 138.

8. Wendell Berry, "To Think of the Life of a Man," *Poetry*, June 1967, Poetry Foundation, https://www.poetryfoundation.org/poetrymagazine/browse?contentId=30632.

9. Robin Wall Kimmerer, *Braiding Sweetgrass: Indigenous Wisdom, Scientific Knowledge, and the Teachings of Plants* (Minneapolis: Milkweed, 2013), 97.

10. Irenaeus, *Against the Heresies*, book 4, chap. 20, accessed October 16, 2023, http://public-library.uk/ebooks/50/2.pdf.

11. N. T. Wright, *Surprised by Hope: Rethinking Heaven, the Resurrection, and the Mission of the Church* (New York: HarperOne, 2018), 158.

12. Lyanda Lynn Haupt, *Rooted: Life at the Crossroads of Science, Nature, and Spirit* (Boston: Little, Brown, 2021), 215.

13. Mary Oliver, "Sleeping in the Forest," *Ohio Review* (Athens: Ohio University, 1978), 49.

14. Norman Wirzba says "liberation into wholeness." Fred Bahnson and Norman Wirzba, *Making Peace with the Land: God's Call to Reconcile with Creation* (Downers Grove, IL: IVP Books, 2012), 27.

15. Madeleine L'Engle, *The Irrational Season* (San Francisco: HarperSanFrancisco, 1995), 109, emphasis added.

16. Joy Harjo, "Remember," in *How We Became Human: New and Selected Poems, 1975–2002* (New York: W. W. Norton, 2002), 42.

17. L'Engle, *Irrational Season*, 3.

18. See Fred Bahnson, *Soil and Sacrament: A Spiritual Memoir of Food and Faith* (New York: Simon & Shuster, 2013), 8.

Chapter 3 Here Is Truth: Land

1. Stanley Plumly, "White Oaks Ascending," in *Poems about Trees*, ed. Harry Thomas (New York: Knopf, 2019), 39.

2. Peter Wohlleben, *The Hidden Life of Trees: What They Feel, How They Communicate—Discoveries from a Secret World* (Glasgow, UK: William Collins, 2017), xi.

3. Robin Wall Kimmerer, *Braiding Sweetgrass: Indigenous Wisdom, Scientific Knowledge, and the Teachings of Plants* (Minneapolis: Milkweed, 2013), 229.

4. The famous line from Whitman's poem "Song of Myself," "I am large, I contain multitudes," can be found in *Leaves of Grass*, first published in 1855.

5. C. S. Lewis, *The Great Divorce* (London: Collins, 1945), viii.

6. Marion Roach Smith, *The Memoir Project: A Thoroughly Non-Standardized Text for Writing and Life* (New York: Grand Central Publishing, 2011), 66.

7. This is the wording of one of Rich Mullins's album titles.

8. Although this saying is sometimes attributed to St. Teresa of Avila, the origin is uncertain.

9. Bessel van der Kolk, *The Body Keeps the Score: Brain, Mind, and Body in the Healing of Trauma* (New York: Penguin Books, 2014), 235.

10. Wendell Berry, "To Think of the Life of a Man," *Poetry*, June 1967, Poetry Foundation, https://www.poetryfoundation.org/poetrymagazine/browse?contentId=30632. Used with permission.

11. Lyanda Lynn Haupt, *Rooted* (Boston: Little, Brown, 2021), 50 (emphasis added).

12. Wendell Berry, "How to Be a Poet," in *New Collected Poems* (Berkeley: Counterpoint, 2012), 354.

Chapter 4 Here Is Hurt: Soil

1. See https://feelingswheel.com.

2. Madeleine L'Engle, *The Irrational Season* (San Francisco: HarperSanFrancisco, 1995), 68.

3. Isak Dinesen, *Seven Gothic Tales* (London: Penguin Books, 1992), 39.

4. I found this quotation, attributed to Reginald Horace Blythe, in a gardening newsletter, *Root Concerns* 13, no. 2 (March 2018), https://s3.amazonaws.com/assets.cce.cornell.edu/attachments/29788/Root_Concerns_MARCH_2018.pdf?1522785490.

5. L'Engle, *Irrational Season*, 34.

6. L'Engle, *Irrational Season*, 56.

7. "Kiss the Ground Film Trailer (2020)," YouTube video, August 20, 2020, 2:29, https://www.youtube.com/watch?v=K3-V1j-zMZw.

8. Susan S. Lang, "'Slow, Insidious' Soil Erosion Threatens Human Health and Welfare as Well as the Environment, Cornell Study Asserts," *Cornell Chronicle*, March 20, 2006, https://news.cornell.edu/stories/2006/03/slow-insidious-soil-erosion-threatens-human-health-and-welfare.

9. "Kiss the Ground Film Trailer (2020)."

10. Wendell Berry, *The Unsettling of America: Culture and Agriculture* (Berkeley: Counterpoint, 2015), 90.

11. Fred Bahnson and Norman Wirzba, *Making Peace with the Land: God's Call to Reconcile with Creation* (Downers Grove, IL: IVP Books, 2012), 16.

12. "Fools and Dreamers: Regenerating a Native Forest," Happen Films, accessed October 18, 2023, https://happenfilms.com/fools-and-dreamers.

13. Terry Tempest Williams, *Erosion: Essays of Undoing* (New York: Sarah Crichton Books, 2019), 116.

14. See Daniel James Ladinsky, *Love Poems from God: Twelve Sacred Voices from the East and West* (New York: Penguin, 2002), 40.

15. Jo Handelsman and Kayla Cohen, *A World without Soil: The Past, Present, and Precarious Future of the Earth beneath Our Feet* (New Haven: Yale University Press, 2022), 23.

Chapter 5 Here Is Grief: Forest Litter

1. Emily Dickinson, "Because I Could Not Stop for Death," Poetry Foundation, https://www.poetryfoundation.org/poems/47652/because-i-could-not-stop-for-death-479.

2. Robert Farrar Capon, *The Supper of the Lamb: A Culinary Reflection* (New York: Modern Library, 2002), 12.

3. C. S Lewis, *A Grief Observed* (London: Crossreach, 2016), 26.

4. Peter Wohlleben and Ruth Ahmedzai Kemp, *Walks in the Wild: A Guide through the Forest* (London: Rider, 2019), 186.

5. See https://recompose.life.

6. Katrina Spade, "Let's Talk about Human Composting, " TEDx Talks, June 16, 2016, YouTube video, 14:05, https://www.youtube.com/watch?v=PRsopS7yTG8.

7. Spade, "Let's Talk about Human Composting," 4:40.

8. Spade, "Let's Talk about Human Composting," 14:27.

9. Rebecca Solnit, *Recollections of My Nonexistence: A Memoir* (New York: Penguin Books, 2020), 32.

10. N. T. Wright, *Surprised by Hope: Rethinking Heaven, the Resurrection, and the Mission of the Church* (New York: HarperOne, 2018), 158.

11. Michael Pollan, *Second Nature: A Gardener's Education* (New York: Grove, 1991), 75.

12. Robin Wall Kimmerer, *Braiding Sweetgrass: Indigenous Wisdom, Scientific Knowledge, and the Teachings of Plants* (Minneapolis: Milkweed, 2013), 327.

13. David Whyte, "Sweet Darkness," *The House of Belonging: Poems* (Langley, WA: Many Rivers, 2011).

14. John O'Donohue, *To Bless the Space between Us: A Book of Blessings* (New York: Doubleday, 2008), 118.

15. Jon R. Luoma, *The Hidden Forest: The Biography of an Ecosystem* (Corvallis: Oregon State University Press, 2006), 68.

16. Diane Langberg, @DianeLangberg, X (formerly Twitter), March 12, 2018, 8:00 a.m., https://twitter.com/DianeLangberg/status/973166850916933637.

17. An audio recording of Dru Johnson making this observation during a talk about rituals is available for purchase from Mars Hill Audio at https://marshillaudio.org/products/mh-149-m#guests.

Chapter 6 Here Is Time: Lichen

1. Robin Wall Kimmerer, *Braiding Sweetgrass: Indigenous Wisdom, Scientific Knowledge, and the Teachings of Plants* (Minneapolis: Milkweed, 2013), 268.

2. Merlin Sheldrake, *Entangled Life: How Fungi Make Our Worlds, Change Our Minds, and Shape Our Futures* (New York: Random House, 2020), 85.

3. Quoted in Melissa Febos, *Body Work* (New York: Catapult, 2022), 26.

4. Sheldrake, *Entangled Life*, 53.

5. *Chef's Table*, season 3, episode 1, "Jeong Kwan," directed by David Gelb, original air date February 17, 2017, on Netflix.

6. Jeff Gordinier, "Jeong Kwan, the Philosopher Chef," *New York Times*, October 16, 2015, https://www.nytimes.com/2015/10/16/t-magazine/jeong-kwan-the-philosopher-chef.html.

7. Gordinier, "Jeong Kwan."

8. Lore Wilbert, "The Hiddenness of Goodness or the Goodness of Hiddenness," Sayable, March 16, 2022, https://www.sayable.net/blog/2022 /3/16/the-hiddenness-of-goodness-or-the-goodness-of-hiddenness.

9. Jane Hirshfield, "For the Lobaria, Usnea, Witches Hair, Map Lichen, Beard Lichen, Ground Lichen, Shield Lichen," Poets.org, accessed September 1, 2023, https://poets.org/poem/lobaria-usnea-witches-hair-map-lichen -beard-lichen-ground-lichen-shield-lichen.

10. Sheldrake, *Entangled Life*, 72.

11. Jon R. Luoma, *The Hidden Forest: The Biography of an Ecosystem* (Corvallis: Oregon State University Press, 2006), 55.

12. Wendell Berry, *The Art of the Commonplace* (New York: Catapult, 2018), 8.

13. Sheldrake, *Entangled Life*, 46.

14. Sheldrake, *Entangled Life*, 46.

15. Frederick Buechner, *Wishful Thinking: A Seeker's ABC* (San Francisco: HarperSanFrancisco, 1993), 119.

16. Denise Levertov, "Overland to the Islands," in *Collected Earlier Poems, 1940–1960* (New York: New Directions, 1979), 55. The bit she borrows from Rilke appears in *Selected Letters of Rainer Maria Rilke, 1902–1926*, trans. R. F. C. Hall (London: Macmillan, 1946), 305.

17. Mary Oliver, *Felicity* (New York: Penguin Books, 2017), 3.

18. Wendell Berry, *The Art of the Commonplace* (New York: Catapult, 2018), xiii.

Chapter 7 Here Is Protection: Nursemaids

1. Quoted in Bill Bryson, *A Walk in the Woods: Rediscovering America on the Appalachian Trail* (New York: Broadway Books, 1998), 45.

2. William Bradford, "1640: A Hideous and Desolate Wilderness," *Lapham's Quarterly*, accessed October 16, 2023, https://www.laphams quarterly.org/book-nature/hideous-and-desolate-wilderness. This is an excerpt from Bradford's journal.

3. Alexis de Tocqueville, "Democracy in America," 1831, https://www .marxists.org/reference/archive/de-tocqueville/democracy-america/ch18 .htm.

4. William Wordsworth, "Nutting," Poetry Foundation, https://www .poetryfoundation.org/poems/45533/nutting.

5. Robin Wall Kimmerer, *Braiding Sweetgrass: Indigenous Wisdom, Scientific Knowledge, and the Teachings of Plants* (Minneapolis: Milkweed, 2013), 283.

6. Rich Mullins, "Here in America," from the album *A Liturgy, a Legacy and a Ragamuffin Band* (Brentwood, TN: Reunion Records, 1993).

7. Richard Powers, *The Overstory* (Toronto: Knopf, 2021), 139.

8. Jon R. Luoma, *The Hidden Forest: The Biography of an Ecosystem* (Corvallis: Oregon State University Press, 2006), 79.

9. Mary Oliver, *Upstream: Selected Essays* (New York: Penguin Books, 2016), 166.

10. Luoma, *Hidden Forest*, 80.

11. "Emma Gannon on Understanding, Not Agreeing," Katherine May, accessed September 1, 2023, https://katherine-may.co.uk/how-we-live-now -season-1/emma-gannon.

12. Curt Thompson, *Soul of Shame* (Downers Grove, IL: InterVarsity, 2015), 138.

13. Wendell Berry, *Fidelity: Five Stories* (New York: Pantheon, 1992), 189.

14. Wendell Berry, *The Art of the Commonplace* (New York: Catapult, 2018), 153.

15. Aldo Leopold, *Sand County Almanac: And Sketches Here and There* (New York: Oxford University Press, 2020), 192.

16. Parker J. Palmer, *A Hidden Wholeness: The Journey toward an Undivided Life: Welcoming the Soul and Weaving Community in a Wounded World* (San Francisco: Jossey-Bass, 2008), 5.

17. Kimmerer, *Braiding Sweetgrass*, 200.

18. Daniel Matthews, *Cascade-Olympic Natural History*, quoted in Sarah Gage, "Nurse Logs," Washington Native Plant Society, November 30, 2020, https://www.wnps.org/blog/nurse-logs.

Chapter 8 Here Is Emergence: Weeds

1. Joan Maloof, *Teaching the Trees: Lessons from the Forest* (Athens: University of Georgia Press, 2007), 82.

2. Michael Pollan, *Second Nature: A Gardener's Education* (New York: Grove Press, 2008), 100.

3. Ralph Waldo Emerson, "Fortune of the Republic," in *The Later Lectures of Ralph Waldo Emerson, 1843–1871*, ed. Joel Myerson and Ronald A. Bosco (Athens: University of Georgia Press, 2010), 2:321.

4. "Look and See: A Portrait of Wendell Berry," a film produced and directed by Laura Dunn and Jef Sewell (Two Birds Film, 2016).

5. Robert B. Shaw, "Moss," *Poetry*, October 1979, Poetry Foundation, https://www.poetryfoundation.org/poetrymagazine/browse?contentId=3 4374.

6. Bruce Guernsey, "Moss," Poetry Foundation, https://www.poetry foundation.org/poems/48004/moss-56d22a563c2d0.

7. Theodore Roethke, "Moss-Gathering," Poetry Foundation, https://www.poetryfoundation.org/poems/153471/moss-gathering.

8. Reggie L. Williams, "Formation for Justice," class lecture given at Friends University, Wichita, Kansas, May 9, 2023.

9. *Merriam-Webster*, s.v. "bushwhack," accessed October 12, 2023, https://www.merriam-webster.com/dictionary/bushwhack.

10. Jon R. Luoma, *The Hidden Forest: The Biography of an Ecosystem* (Corvallis: Oregon State University Press, 2006), 30.

11. Henry David Thoreau, "Walking," *Atlantic*, June 1, 1862, https://www.theatlantic.com/magazine/archive/1862/06/walking/304674/.

Chapter 9 Here Is Resilience: Mycelia

1. Suzanne Simard, *Finding the Mother Tree: Discovering the Wisdom of the Forest* (New York: Knopf, 2021), 202.

2. Simard, *Finding the Mother Tree*, 60.

3. Simard, *Finding the Mother Tree*, 160.

4. Jon R. Luoma, *The Hidden Forest: The Biography of an Ecosystem* (Corvallis: Oregon State University Press, 2006), 58.

5. "Derrick Jensen: How the West Has Won," Films for Action, accessed September 1, 2023, https://www.filmsforaction.org/watch/derrick-jensen -how-the-west-has-won/.

6. Simard, *Finding the Mother Tree*, 145.

7. Simard, *Finding the Mother Tree*, 160.

8. Simard, *Finding the Mother Tree*, 281 (emphasis added).

9. W. H. Auden, "Woods," in *The Complete Works of W. H. Auden*, vol. 2, *Poems*, ed. Edward Mendelson (Princeton: Princeton University Press, 2022), 408.

10. Robin Wall Kimmerer, *Braiding Sweetgrass: Indigenous Wisdom, Scientific Knowledge, and the Teachings of Plants* (Minneapolis: Milkweed, 2013), 338.

11. Luoma, *Hidden Forest*, 122.

12. Simard, *Finding the Mother Tree*, 224.

13. Lyanda Lynn Haupt, *Rooted: Life at the Crossroads of Science, Nature, and Spirit* (Boston: Little, Brown, 2021), 172.

14. Elizabeth Barrett Browning, *Aurora Leigh and Other Poems* (1856; repr., London: Penguin Books, 2006), 232.

Chapter 10 Here Is Movement: Forest

1. M. Amos Clifford, *Your Guide to Forest Bathing: Experience the Healing Power of Nature* (Newburyport, MA: Conari, 2018), 2.

2. Albert W. Palmer, "A Parable of Sauntering," Sierra Club, September 27, 2023, https://vault.sierraclub.org/john_muir_exhibit/life/palmer_saunter ing.aspx. Excerpt from his book *The Mountain Trail and Its Message* (Cleveland: Pilgrim Press, 1911).

3. Henry David Thoreau, "Walking," *Atlantic*, June 1, 1862, https://www.theatlantic.com/magazine/archive/1862/06/walking/304674.

4. Pádraig Ó. Tuama, *In the Shelter: Finding a Home in the World* (Minneapolis: Broadleaf Books, 2021), 8.

5. Chaim Potok, *The Gift of Asher Lev* (New York: Fawcett Columbine, 1997), 118.

6. Philip Larkin, "The Trees," in *Poems about Trees*, ed. Harry Thomas (New York: Knopf, 2019), 239.

7. Gerard Manley Hopkins, "Binsey Poplars," in Thomas, *Poems about Trees*, 170.

8. Susan Orlean, "The Tallest Known Tree in New York Falls in the Forest," *New Yorker*, January 18, 2022, https://www.newyorker.com/news/afterword/the-tallest-known-tree-in-new-york-falls-in-the-forest.

9. Rainer Maria Rilke, *Duino Elegies*, trans. David Oswald (Switzerland: Daimon Verlag, 1997), 91.

10. Madeleine L'Engle, *The Irrational Season* (San Francisco: HarperSanFrancisco, 1995), 3.

11. William Butler Yeats, "The Second Coming," Poetry Foundation, https://www.poetryfoundation.org/poems/43290/the-second-coming.

12. Annie Stoltie, "Looking Up," *Adirondack Life*, December 2020, https://www.adirondacklife.com/2020/11/03/looking-up/.

LORE FERGUSON WILBERT (MA, Friends University) is the author of *A Curious Faith* and *Handle with Care*, which won a 2021 *Christianity Today* Book Award. She has written for *Christianity Today*, *Fathom* magazine, and She Reads Truth and served as general editor of B&H's Read and Reflect with the Classics. She lives on the edge of the Adirondack Mountains in Upstate New York with her husband, Nate.

CONNECT WITH LORE:

www.lorefergusonwilbert.com

 lorewilbert.com

Lore Ferguson Wilbert

@lorewilbert